READING THE UNSEEN

READING THE UNSEEN

DENVER 2010

For Alicia —
" welcome to [mills]
/ Elsinore — !

(Offstage) *Hamlet*

Stephen Ratcliffe

All best wishes
Stephen Ratcliffe

4 . 1 . 11

COUNTERPATH PRESS

For John, Lepai, Oona & Johnny

Counterpath Press
Denver, Colorado
www.counterpathpress.org

Printed in Canada

Library of Congress Cataloging-in-Publication Data

Ratcliffe, Stephen.
  Reading the unseen : (offstage) Hamlet / Stephen Ratcliffe.
    p. cm.
  Includes bibliographical references and index.
  ISBN 978-1-933996-14-1 (pbk. : alk. paper)
  1. Shakespeare, William, 1564–1616. 2. Hamlet. I. Title.
PR2807.R37   2010
822.3'3—dc22
                                    2009028174

Distributed by Small Press Distribution (www.spdbooks.org)

Contents

Acknowledgments

I'm surprised it's taken me so long to write such a short and also improbable book—improbable because *Hamlet* has already had so much written about it even though my subject (offstage action in the play) has hardly been noticed. I must have first become aware of "offstage action" over forty years ago, when I played the part of the old man Giles Corey in Burlingame High School's production of Arthur Miller's *The Crucible* (when I was pressed to death, offstage of course, my last defiant words were reported to have been "more weight"). Some thirty years later, I wrote an essay on Gertrude's speech on Ophelia's death, seeing it not as an instance of offstage action but rather as a 16-line "poem" whose words seemed to open up to the possibilities of close reading. Thereafter, over a period of years, followed a series of essays—one called "'Shakespeare' and 'I'" (now the Afterword), one on the Ghost's speech, one on the opening lines of the play, all of them leading me to think further about the presence and significance of the action that isn't performed in the play (except in words).

I owe great thanks to a number people for their help along the way: Stephen Booth, for first showing me the possibilities of close reading; Judith Anderson, for her reading of an earlier version of the entire book; Margreta de Grazia and Cornelia Nixon, for their responses to earlier versions of Chapter Five; David Bernstein, for his thoughts on the Preface; Patricia Parker, Janet Adelman, Harry Berger, Jr., Stephen Orgel, Ulla Dydo, Charles Bernstein, and Lyn Hejinian, for their ongoing offstage presence; Robert Grenier, for an also ongoing onstage conversation ("speech") that has meant more to me than I can acknowledge here; Allen Shoaf of *Exemplaria* and Stephen Foley of *Modern Language Studies*, where earlier versions of several chapters first appeared; and Tim Roberts and Julie Carr of Counterpath, without whose initial belief in it (and meticulous work on its behalf), *Reading the Unseen* would not have come into this world.

Bolinas, California
July 30, 2009

Preface

This book is about offstage action in *Hamlet*, about words that describe action that isn't performed physically in the play, things we don't actually see: King Hamlet's murder in his orchard, Ophelia's death in the stream, Hamlet's visit to Ophelia's closet, Hamlet's voyage to England, and so on. I focus on *Hamlet* because it is the most celebrated and enigmatic of all Shakespeare's plays and because it among all of Shakespeare's plays is the one that most fully explores the dramatic possibilities, limits, and implications of offstage action.[1] In looking at speeches that refer to such "invisible" action—the Ghost's speech about how Claudius poured the "juice of cursed hebona . . . in the porches of my ears"[2] (1.5.62), Gertrude's speech about how Ophelia "Fell in the weeping brook" (4.7.173), Ophelia's speech about how Hamlet appeared in her "closet . . . with his doublet all unbraced, / No hat upon his head" (2.1.77–78), Hamlet's speech about how he jumped "Up from my cabin, my sea gown scarfed about me, in the dark" (5.2.12–13)—I want to think about how the "Words, words, words" (2.2.192) in these speeches work to make physically absent things imaginatively "present;" how they "show" us action we don't actually see;

how what is concealed from us (thus unseen, unknown) is essential both to this play and to our lives in this world—beyond which lies the ultimate unknown, that "undiscovered country/From whose bourn no traveler returns" (3.1.79–80).

To say *Hamlet* is about its "Words, words, words" is not to say it is not also a play about performed physical things. The representation or mimesis of physical action that we do not see performed in the play, only hear about in its words, is not separate from its physical action: words and action are completely intertwined. Both literal and physical are central to the play, the ear and eye essential to how we get it perceptually, and know it. Words are also physical things; sound also; so too is the act of speaking. The materialities both of language and of physical action performed on a stage are alike, though also obviously very different. Because the relation between onstage and offstage things is also in effect seamless, the question becomes: What, conceptually, is the play doing with language? What is the reader, or member of an audience, doing? And how are these doings related? The plot of *Hamlet* raises such questions, and guides and constrains my reading of the play, as does my sense of how language works (whether Shakespeare himself thought of such things, one can only guess). Another question comes to mind: does the seamlessness of what is performed in word and deed onstage include deeds (physical, visible) whose meanings are multiple or unclear (even as linguistic events are)? What are the epistemological differences between these ambiguous events and linguistically ambiguous events? (Hamlet sees Claudius praying for example, but what he sees is deceptive.)

In thinking about offstage action in *Hamlet*, I will focus on what happens in and on the level of the play's language. The words I will talk about are the words spoken by actors when the play is performed onstage, the ones we hear when we watch and listen to the play being performed. But the things I will talk about are not the things that audiences watching and listening to the play will notice, not because they are not there but because the performance of the play happens too quickly, takes place in the more or less "two hours' traffic of our stage" that it takes to perform the play, whereas the things I talk about in *Hamlet* can only be noticed in reading words on the page—what Harry Berger, Jr. has called "armchair interpretation."[3]

My own "armchair" reading of *Hamlet* pays close attention to the "action" of its words—that is, to the semantic, phonetic, grammatical and ideational interrelationships between "words, words, words" in the play, many of which are unlikely to be noticed by an audience watching and listening to *Hamlet* being performed in the theater. It is a reading that begins, as Patricia Parker puts it, "with the conviction that careful or close reading is not the preserve of the ahistorical or apolitical"[4]—nor I think the atheatrical, since my concerns in reading the words of *Hamlet* on the page are always to see them, or rather hear and understand them, as words performed by actors on a stage—words that refer to things that are not performed on that stage except in those words. It also recognizes that reading words on a page and hearing actors speaking words aloud from a stage are two different kinds of experiences—one of seeing words with the eyes, the other listening with the ears; one private, the other public; one that can slow down and also interrupt the play's forward motion, the other that is swept along by it; one that allows us to think at leisure about the intricacies of the performed text, the other that dazzles us with what Berger, Jr. calls its "spell."[5]

As such, my "armchair" reading explores what David Scott Kastan has called "the necessity of reading"[6]—reading *Hamlet*'s words that is, and in so doing, thinking about things that will not ordinarily be noticed (by audiences watching and listening to *Hamlet* in the theater at least). Slowing down our experience of the play, I pay attention to how its words (a continuously unfolding series of verbal actions) make meanings in interaction with each other as elements of a work whose surfaces extend in all dimensions, spatial as well as temporal, and whose complex multiplicity of parts function in multiple systems of order simultaneously. The play I am reading is therefore not the play an audience is watching in the theater but an idea of that play, or, as I would like to think of it, that ideal play—the one that Shakespeare wrote.[7]

To claim that in my reading of *Hamlet* I am reading the play "that Shakespeare wrote" is likely to raise questions from critics who point out, as Kastan writes, that Shakespeare's "literary career strikingly resists the very notions of artistic authority and autonomy that his name has come triumphantly to represent." Shakespeare's plays were indeed collaborative and social ventures, and in reading the words of *Hamlet* I do not mean to ignore what Kastan calls "the historically specific conditions of its writing and circulation" but rather to understand it in the light of its offstage action, which is also not present except in words. That is to say, like the "conditions" that Kastan would discover about "the historicity of the play . . . its production and reception . . . marks of this worldliness . . . materializations . . . [which] are its meanings,"[8] *Hamlet*'s offstage action is also missing—its "absence" made present in the play-text performed by actors, witnessed by audiences, read by the play's readers, all of whom participate in and thus help to perpetuate and realize the play's "worldliness" as well as its "meanings."

Thus thinking about the differences between text vs. performance, reading vs. playgoing, the autonomy of an "author" vs. the uncertainty of collective production, my "armchair" reading is related to what may be called the fictions of reading.[9] We can imagine ourselves reading as if listening to a speech, conversation, or story; we can imagine ourselves reading as if looking at a picture, play, film, or sequence of events; we can imagine ourselves reading as if perusing—that is, producing and constructing—a text. Reading is always reading-as-if, which is only to repeat the outworn and politically correct (but still correct) view that reading is always a socially constructed practice, that is, a convention, like the writing that reproduces and represents it. Different kinds of texts—arrangements of words—can nudge us toward one or another or some combination of these fictions of reading. The question is how some passages not only refer to offstage phenomena but represent them in a way that invites us to visualize them or makes it hard for us to visualize them, and thus function as both metaphoric interpretations of the speech acts they appear in and words themselves—which are never the same thing as the physical action they describe. The payoff in approaching the speeches I will look at is that we are able to see the relation between what is being described (offstage action) and the language that describes it—a relation between language (words read on the page, or heard when spoken into the air) and the physical event that language means to "show," that is, represent.

Thinking further about reading as a form of looking at pictures, it may also be useful to think about the play's offstage action in relation to visual arts, specifically to painting and film. I look at Jan van Eyck's painting *Giovanni Arnolfini and His Bride* in Chapter Five, for example, as an image suggesting not only the absent presence of Shakespeare the author and the setting of offstage action in *Hamlet*, but also Ophelia herself, who might (like the woman in van Eyck's painting) be pregnant. (I say "might" not because I believe Ophelia is pregnant—Shakespeare gives us no real evidence to suggest that she is—but because I want to point to how much of *Hamlet* happens offstage without any evidence of exactly what does take place or who is responsible for what, thus complicating the question of "evidence" itself—e.g., of epistemology and knowing, showing and the difficulty of seeing beyond "show," the unknowableness of what isn't seen, etc.) In Chapter Four I look at how the words of Gertrude's speech "show" Ophelia's death—an offstage, unseen death that is also shown in John Everett Millais's great painting "Ophelia," whose slow-motion, static feeling of calm suggests something of the distance, the displacement and diffusion, that physical actions "painted" in words appear to have in *Hamlet*. Hamlet's spoken and written words to Horatio "show" us what happened offstage on his voyage to England, which I talk about in Chapter Two: how he "fingered" Rosencrantz and Guildenstern's "packet"; how "a pirate of very warlike appointment gave us chase," later how "in the grapple" he "boarded them" and thus was able to make his way back to Elsinore (all of this unseen in Shakespeare's play but filmed in Olivier's *Hamlet*). So too with Shakespeare's own written words, which are all we have to "show" us who Shakespeare the man really was, that person who has disappeared into his words despite an engraved image on the First Folio's title page, which I talk about in relation to the missing (offstage) author and his missing offstage action in my Afterword. Such disappearance of physical action (or Shakespeare) into words, representing what we do not see onstage (although Olivier films it) might be seen as a kind of verbal camouflage, *Hamlet*'s language removing its physical action into the "background" of its textual surface so to speak, where we can no longer see it, can only hear verbal references to it. The poet John Ashbery suggests a similar disappearing trick in Cubism, which like camouflage "obliterates by pressing a thing as far as possible back into the waves of otherness that surround it"[10]—"otherness" in this case not paint but language itself, Hamlet's words at certain points "indistinguishable" from its physical action. But in this disappearance into the play's language, physical things we might otherwise see (were they performed onstage) take upon themselves a kind of visual resonance, echo, or presence established, and also conveyed to us, in words that deliver (even though the things those words refer to are not-seen, not-seeable) something more informative than any performed action, what T. J. Clark, also writing about Picasso's Cubism, imagines when he says "The moment of maximum visual information in a picture is that at which the object goes out of sight"[11]: the "object" here again not paint but character, who disappears from the play's stage into its words (Hamlet's father's account of his death in the orchard, his mother's account of Ophelia's death in the stream).

Lest anyone imagine that the kinds of things I will think about in *Hamlet* happen only in *Hamlet*, let me make it clear that Shakespeare's plays are full of things we do not see, things performed in words only. Othello's tale of how he won Desdemona's love, Enobarbus's account of how Antony met Cleopatra on the barge, Prospero's history of how he and Miranda first arrived on the island: this prehistory is essential to our understanding of the play's present action—as is the Ghost's speech to Hamlet about how he was murdered, which I will talk about further in Chapter Three. Still other action previous to the play's present actions is referred to in more casual but still memorable ways: a bleeding Captain's "report" of Macbeth carving Macdonwald "from the nave to th' chaps" (1.2.1–22), Orlando complaining of mistreatment by an older brother in *As You Like It*, Orsino's confession of love sickness for Olivia in *Twelfth Night*, Gloucester's recollection of his "sport" (1.1.22) in "making" his bastard son in *King Lear*: these and hundreds of other instances elsewhere of how, in their opening lines, Shakespeare's plays "show" us bits and pieces of things we do not see performed physically onstage—things we probably do not notice we have heard listening to the play—as do the opening lines of *Hamlet*, which I will look at in Chapter One. Happening offstage during the time of the play, still other events are described by someone who has witnessed (or heard about) them: Edgar's story of how Gloucester's heart "'Twixt two extremes of passion, joy and grief/Burst smilingly" (5.3.190–91) in *King Lear* (which would certainly be difficult for any actor to perform physically onstage), Egypt's Queen recalling how Antony's "legs bestrid the ocean, his reared arm/Crested the world" (5.2.83–84) in *Antony and Cleopatra* (more than difficult to perform), the Gentleman describing Leontes meeting his daughter at the end of *The Winter's Tale* (which "undoes description to do it" [5.2.57] and could not be performed onstage, at least not realistically, not that realism is ever on Shakespeare's list of dramatic requirements)—all these instances of action we do not see performed physically onstage (perhaps because they cannot be performed) but instead "shown" in words the play uses to describe those actions.

Finally, recent attention to the problem of knowing the authentic Shakespearean text might be taken to suggest that one's attempt to read the words of a play by Shakespeare, particularly one like *Hamlet*, which exists in three separate versions (the First Quarto, the Second Quarto, and the Folio) as well as any number of modern edited editions, no two of which are exactly alike, is likely to run aground on the sharp rocks of indeterminacy.[12] Choosing to read the words of *Hamlet* in *The Complete Pelican Shakespeare*, taking them as one of several possible versions of a work whose "authentic" version cannot be known, I mean both to acknowledge the essential indeterminacy of the play's material text and to propose that offstage action may be understood in terms of it: that is, the constructed text whose absent or "missing" original does not exist (cannot be performed or even seen, can only be speculated about) may be taken to stand for or represent—literally to enact—the physical absence of the play's "missing'" offstage action, action that can only be speculated about (whether heard by the play's audience or read by its readers), action performed in the "Words, words, words" that I (like Hamlet himself) will be reading. And in suggesting such a parallel between reading in the play (Hamlet's) and reading of the play (my "armchair" reading), I want also to suggest that the physically "missing" offstage action about which we as readers and audience can only speculate may be understood in relation to the ghostly presence of the "missing" author, "Shakespeare" himself, who is indeed also "offstage," about whom we know so little other than his words—"inauthentic" as they may be, some of which (the ones that dramatize its offstage action) refer to "missing" things, things we must speculate about from the words Shakespeare uses to describe or, as I would say, "perform" them.

READING THE UNSEEN

1

"Who's There?" (I):
Elsinore and Elsewhere

The first half of my title is meant to suggest a "knock knock" joke, one that goes something like this:

> "Knock knock."
> "Who's there?"
> "Nay, answer me."
> "Nay, answer me who?"
> "Nay, answer me. Stand and unfold yourself?"

And so the play continues, beginning with a question whose significance resonates through *Hamlet*: who/what is "there"? Barnardo is not joking of course, and yet his line *is* a response to some implied, unspoken physical action—Francisco scraping his lance or foot?—which Barnardo has seen and/or heard.[1] "[T]here" points to the castle walls at Elsinore and to the stage itself (Barnardo, entering from offstage, asks Francisco, who is already onstage, "Who's *there*?"), but it also implies an offstage "elsewhere," both sentinels keeping eyes and ears open for someone, or something, "there": the ghost of Hamlet's father whose "dreaded sight" they have now "twice seen," his action "there" what their words will talk about here. Indeed, from this opening forward clear through to the end,

Hamlet is focused on things "elsewhere": actions not performed physically "there," onstage—things we only hear about in words, things we must therefore imagine and speculate about.[2]

Calling attention to the relation between *words*, which we hear, and *action*, which we see (or if not see, then hear about), Barnardo's question "Who's there?" sets the stage for what I want to think about here: the relation between onstage and offstage action in the play's opening lines, whose attention to things not physically shown make them a microcosm of the entire play. All of Shakespeare's plays, indeed all plays, spend a certain amount of time telling us about what is not seen (because it is not performed physically, is "shown" only in "messenger speeches," among the oldest of all dramatic devices[3]) but *Hamlet* goes further than any other play by Shakespeare—perhaps than any other play—in exploring the differences between showing and telling, what we can know because we see it with our eyes and what we must speculate about or imagine because we only hear about it in the words the play uses to describe it (the words our ears "tell" us about it). Why Shakespeare pushed further into the unperformed and thus unknown, unrepresentable world of offstage action in *Hamlet* we can only guess.[4] What we can say with certainty is that nearly everything in the play—all of its onstage, performed, observable action—derives from and is focused on action that took place *before* the play's performed action: the action of King Hamlet's murder in his orchard, Gertrude's possible adultery and also complicity in that murder—things we are told that took place in what Patricia Parker has called "an offstage primal scene beyond the reach of vision . . . an offstage secret the entire play comes belatedly after and then attempts recursively to bring to light."[5] Which is not only to say that everything in *Hamlet* happens *after* what has happened before the play begins but also that everything in the play reaches outward, away from what is being performed onstage, toward the unseen, unknown, and unknowable offstage world, what Hamlet, speaking not of offstage action but death, calls "[t]he undiscovered country, from whose bourn/No traveler returns" (3.1.79–80): death being the ultimate offstage action, which is perhaps why Shakespeare became so obsessed with the performance of offstage action in *Hamlet*, whose Ghost (it seems to be Shakespeare's invention, since there is no Ghost in any of his sources) may be taken to represent ("perform," literally to embody) everything we cannot see (and thereby know) in this world.

The relation between *seeing* action and only *hearing* about it raises questions about the nature of our experience in the theater. What is the difference between physical and verbal "action"? What happens when words call attention to action that happens elsewhere, offstage, in words only? How do we know what *really* happened if we don't see it performed physically onstage, only hear of it? How do we move so easily back and forth between things we see being performed physically onstage and things we hear about in words but do not see—except to the extent that we "see" them in words that "describe," as Wittgenstein says, "how things are"?[6] "[I]s the thing seen or the thing heard," as Gertrude Stein asks,

the thing that makes most of its impression upon you at the theatre, and does as the scene in the theatre proceeds does the hearing take the place of seeing as perhaps it does when something real is being most exciting, or does seeing take the place of hearing as perhaps it does when anything real is happening or does the mixture get to be more mixed seeing and hearing as perhaps it does when anything really exciting is really happening.[7]

What Stein calls the "mixture" between seeing and hearing is intrinsic to our experience of plays of the theater. Actors moving around onstage performing the play's present business ask us to focus on a series of continuously present moments of theatrical time, moments coincident with the time it takes the actors to perform the play and us in the audience to witness it. Actors moving around onstage talking about past or future or present but unseen action ask us to imagine something in another time and place.[8] Such interruption is not, in the theater at least, surprising, nor are we even slightly disturbed to find our attention so split apart. Even if we tried to separate something seen onstage from something talked about but not seen, we would find it difficult; the curtain between what happens onstage and what happens offstage is in effect seamless.

Things "missing" from *Hamlet*, events performed only in the words the Ghost speaks when he tells Hamlet how he was murdered, for example, move the play elsewhere, away from physical actions being performed onstage—by actors playing the parts of characters themselves made of words[9]—toward a world of verbal action, which represents the play's missing events but also fails to make them visibly present. The play's "failure" at any such point— the failure of its performance of words to "show" the physical things that they talk about—may be understood as the offspring of a marriage between two different systems of meaning (one in words, one gestures) whose coherence amounts to an accumulation of incoherences.[10] Words that sound centrifugally outward, moving away from the stage toward an "elsewhere" beyond the space of the play's physical action (which is itself "echoed" in the play's verbal performance of that action), "show" us only a literally verbal world, one whose events we are invited to "see" and believe—what "really" happened in the orchard—in the offstage world that *Hamlet*'s words nonetheless fail to make physically present "here" (or rather "there") onstage. The history of the world that does not enter the play—offstage, elsewhere, imagined, not seeable, "missing in action"—would be entirely lost were it not for the play's words, whose "evidence," calling it into the verbal space of the air that actors, when they speak, breathe into and fill, will always remain suspect because it isn't "shown"; is therefore always mysterious, uncertain, unknown and unknowable, unverifiable, always subject to speculation, doubt, interpretation and reinterpretation, as the history of *Hamlet* indeed testifies.

The verbal presence of "missing," physically unperformed action scarcely seems improbable if we think about how *Hamlet* is, for viewers as well as readers, both a play and "an improbable fiction," as Fabian in *Twelfth Night* puts it.[11] *Hamlet* is "improbable" because it asks us to believe things that we know to be false: that a ghost really walks on the castle walls at Elsinore, that Hamlet really stabs Polonius through the arras, that the bodies onstage at the end of the play really are dead, that the actors really are the characters they pretend to be.[12] It is also a fiction, in that it presents a story rather than fact, one that must be "imagined"—by the reader, actor, audience—from the words it uses to "tell" that story: "The king died, and then the queen died of grief," as E. M. Forster put it,[13] distinguishing "story" from "plot" and thinking perhaps of the play whose hero calls "fiction . . . a *dream* of passion" (2.2.490, italics mine).

In order to demonstrate the presence of a multitude of mostly unnoticed (in the theater at least; they *can* be noticed in an "armchair" reading of the play's words on the page, although, aside from some exceptions noted in what follows, they have not been noticed, as far as I know, prior to my reading here) instances of offstage action *throughout Hamlet*, I want now to look at the opening lines of the play. I realize, of course, that any play must paint in the "background"—what happened before the play began—before it can go forward; *Hamlet*, in this regard at least, is not unusual. I do mean to insist, however, that the "insignificance" of the things that I point to here is itself significant; indeed, unnoticed things are essential in *Hamlet* because they show us that what we do *not* see, therefore cannot *ever* know or be entirely certain of, is nonetheless present in the words that are themselves "evidence" of those things they are a "trace" of—words by means of which, in their "failure" to represent (literally "embody," make physically present) the "missing" things they report, Shakespeare stages what Harry Berger, Jr. calls "characteristic limits of the medium."[14]

Here then is an account of the actions we hear about but do not actually see performed onstage in the opening lines of *Hamlet*: "Who's there?" (1.1.1) calls us to attention by calling our attention away from the speaker (Barnardo) toward someone else: both Francisco, who stands on the same stage (Elsinore), and the Ghost, whom Barnardo and Francisco "two nights have seen" (and will soon see again tonight), who is himself standing offstage ("elsewhere") waiting to enter at line 39. Because his question comes as a response to some real or imagined action—Francisco scraping his lance, the absent Ghost whose presence in the dark Barnardo fears he has seen ("this dreaded sight") or heard ("not a mouse stirring")—it also calls attention to what has happened before the play itself begins. And because he has entered the play to replace Francisco, who has been standing watch until now (and who, one might think, as the guard still on duty, should be the one to ask such a question),[15] his question is directed not only to the theatrical space of the stage where Francisco stands but also to "there," which represents some location "elsewhere," some distant place occupied by the third person signified by a subject "Who" in a question crucial to the entire play: "Who's there?"—who, or what, are you? "What art thou?" (1.1.46) as Horatio asks the Ghost (which is what Hamlet asks of nearly everyone: the Ghost, Gertrude, Claudius, Polonius, Ophelia, Fortinbras, Rosencrantz and Guildenstern, Laertes, the Player who weeps for Hecuba). It is also the question most of these same characters ask of Hamlet:

"How is it that the clouds still hang on you?" (1.2.66); "How does my good Lord Hamlet?" (2.2.171); "How does your honor for this many a day?" (3.1.91); "Good my lord, What is the cause of your distemper?" (3.2.330–31); "Alas, how is't with you, / That you do bend your eye on vacancy, / And with th' incorporal air do hold discourse?" (3.4.117–18). It is also what we ask, not only of Hamlet but of Shakespeare himself.

Francisco's reply, "Nay, answer me. Stand and unfold yourself" (1.1.2), first in its refusal to answer Barnardo's question ("Who's there?") and then its command that Barnardo "unfold yourself," sets into motion a series of events, both physical and verbal, that do not take place in the play.[16] We will not (indeed cannot) witness that "unfold[ing]" by which Barnardo would turn himself physically inside out, as if such an act—a gesture that the actor who plays Barnardo will not perform—might reveal the identity of the man Francisco's order means to discover. Nor will we hear Barnardo tell Francisco exactly what "unfold yourself" seems to ask for.

Barnardo's "Long live the King!" (1.1.3) also points to a person, time, and place we cannot see onstage. We do not know which king he means, and the fact that Denmark's former king was recently murdered (an event that happens in an orchard we never see, before the play we are watching has begun) gives a decidedly ironic spin to Barnardo's perhaps wholly conventional cry.[17] The long life called for here will of course take place elsewhere and in other time—far away from what we see being performed onstage at this moment.

The next pair of lines, Francisco's "Barnardo?" and Barnardo's "He" (4–5), complement one another in the potential, but also actual, misunderstandings they suggest. Directed toward the man who has just appeared onstage, Francisco's "Barnardo" sounds as though it could be the name of the king (offstage) to whom

Barnardo has just wished a long life. But "Barnardo" is the name not of the king but of the man who is about to stand watch for the king, the man who in answer to his name being called out responds not with the first person ("I") but third person ("He"), a shift that invites our attention away from the person he is—the person onstage—toward someone else who is now offstage, perhaps again the unnamed king.

Francisco's "You come most carefully upon your hour" (1.1.6) again invites us to think about things other than what is now taking place onstage: Where has Barnardo come from? What has he been doing? Why is he being so careful in this, the appointed hour of his coming?

Barnardo's reply, "'Tis now struck twelve. Get thee to bed, Francisco" (1.1.7), modulates a space between an absolutely present moment sounded by the clock (which is now sounding offstage) and an immediate future elsewhere, during which time Francisco will sleep in a bed we cannot now see (it is offstage) and will in fact never see, though other beds (most importantly Gertrude's) will later figure the play.[18] "Get[ting] thee to bed" will also be echoed later in the play, when Hamlet repeatedly orders Ophelia to "Get thee to a nunnery," a place (or rather pair of places—convent and brothel—neither of which appears in the play) in which a bed plays an important part.

Francisco's reply, "For this relief much thanks. 'Tis bitter cold, / And I am sick at heart" (1.1.8–9), again defines two distinct spaces, one the visible "here" (represented onstage as the castle at Elsinore) and one the invisible (and unrepresentable) "elsewhere" of the interior of Francisco's body—an "unperformable" (except in words) interior that is performed in the Ghost's speech about how poison "course[d] through / The natural gates and alleys of [his] body," whose metaphoric heart "sick[ness]" stands metonymically for the disease that plagues all of Denmark.[19]

Barnardo's next question followed by Francisco's reply, "Have you had a quiet guard?" "Not a mouse stirring" (1.1.10), again asks us to focus on what has taken place offstage, prior to the present action now being performed. We have not witnessed the time of Francisco's "guard"—do not understand why he is keeping watch at this point, though we assume that he and Barnardo must know that. Nor do we hear or see the "mouse" that Francisco has not heard or seen "stirring" during his watch, an offstage mouse (all castles have them) that will later appear onstage, transformed into Hamlet's play *The Mousetrap*, "the image of a murder done in Vienna" (3.2.234)—a place that is also "elsewhere," far away from the image of the court at Elsinore now being performed onstage.[20]

Barnardo's next lines, "Well, good night./If you do meet Horatio and Marcellus,/The rivals of my watch, bid them make haste" (1.1.11–13), once again stand as a bridge between what we see taking place onstage and what we are asked to imagine will or might take place "elsewhere" later. The conditional "If you do meet Horatio and Marcellus" suggests that such a meeting will only take place after Francisco has walked offstage, somewhere else in the future of a world we have not yet seen—nor will we ever see it—in which his words will "bid" those "rivals of [Barnardo's] watch" to hurry to the place where the play's present action is now being performed onstage.

Francisco's reply to this request, "I think I hear them. Stand, ho! Who is there?" (1.1.14), immediately sets into motion the meeting Barnardo has assumed will take place elsewhere. The sound of voices or movement that Francisco thinks he hears comes from offstage, out of sight of the two characters who perform the changing of the guard and of the audience who watches and listens to them engaged in that performance.[21] Francisco's command that Horatio and Marcellus "Stand" draws our attention to where they do stand—upstage or downstage left or right or center, depending on how the actors play the scene. "Stand" followed by "Who is there," in echoing Barnardo's "Who's there?" followed by Francisco's "Stand and unfold yourself" (1.1.1–2), calls our attention to events that have taken place in the play prior to now, verbal events in this case whose presence (already-in-the-past) enact the physics of the play's continuously present unfolding of words. "There" is of course elsewhere, not "here," though perhaps at this point onstage (depending again on how the actors choose to play it). Finally, the words "I think I hear" suggest two separate offstage "scenes," both of them unperformable onstage except in words: first, the interior of Francisco's ear, which "hear[s] them"—an ear that will appear twenty-four times in the play in other places and bodies, most prominently the Ghost's; second, a mental space in which Francisco "think[s]" he has "hear[d] them"—both of these actions taking place onstage only to the extent that we can imagine them in the words used to perform them.

Horatio's and Marcellus's shared line, "Friends to this ground. And liegemen to the Dane" (1.1.15), again defines a pair of spaces, one onstage ("this ground") and the other off ("the Dane" suggests the king who represents the whole of his country). Horatio's word "Friends" suggests (although we do not of course know this yet) his long friendship with Hamlet—all of which has taken place offstage before the play begins. "[L]iegemen" (Marcellus-the-soldier being one of them, having earned the right to that name by virtue of his prior actions "elsewhere"), conjures up the whole political history of Denmark, none of which we have seen though we hear something about it soon enough, in Horatio's account of how King Hamlet "slay[ed] this Fortinbras" (1.1.86) whose son, marching with a "list of lawless resolutes" (98) against Denmark, is the reason these soldiers now stand watch in this place.

Francisco and Marcellus share the next line, "Give you good

night. O, farewell, honest soldier" (1.1.16), which shows us Francisco's character and defines two different places and times. In wishing his friends "good night," Francisco of course means this night; "Farewell, honest soldier," on the other hand, calls our attention away from what is being performed onstage, toward both the "elsewhere" Francisco will arrive at once he leaves the stage and those offstage actions (prior to those now being performed) that have proved him an "honest soldier."

Several words in the next pair of half-lines, "Who hath relieved you?" and "Barnardo hath my place" (1.1.17), echo words from previous lines: "Who" in lines 1 and 14, "relief" in line 8, and "Barnardo" in line 4—thereby working to explore the discontinuous continuousness of present time and present verbal action. Repeating the idea (but not language) of Horatio's "this ground," Francisco's "place"—meaning here "role" as watch or guard as well as ground upon which such a person stands—signals not only his present location but the interchange of persons (one who comes from "elsewhere," one who leaves for "elsewhere") presently taking place in this place. (Notice too what we don't notice in the theater—that this "Who" [i.e., Barnardo] is neither the one in Barnardo's "Who's there?" [i.e., Francisco, or, since Barnardo might well imagine he has heard him, the Ghost] nor the one in Francisco's "Who is there?" [i.e., Horatio and Marcellus, who have just entered]—a shift in referent as easily missed as the slippage between on- and offstage action, which we also don't notice.)

The next line, divided between Francisco ("Give you good night"), Marcellus ("Holla, Barnardo!") and Barnardo ("Say—"), once again directs our attention to what is taking place offstage as well as on. Francisco's last words before leaving his "place" on-stage look both backward into the past—they repeat his words to Marcellus in line 16—and forward into the future—they wish a "good night" for the two guards who have come on duty and, by extension, for himself who now leaves the present scene, presumably to retire to his bed. Marcellus's "Holla, Barnardo!" in turn echoes Francisco's "Barnardo?" in line 3—there a question, here an exclamation; there the guard standing watch calling to the one who enters from "elsewhere," here the one who enters from "elsewhere" calling to the one now standing watch at Elsinore.

Whereas the words of Marcellus and Barnardo that make up the rest of line 18 ("Holla, Barnardo! / Say—") are aimed at people and present action onstage, the following line, divided between Barnardo's "What, is Horatio there?" and Horatio's "A piece of him" (19), once again calls our attention away from what we see and hear being performed onstage. As it did in lines 1 and 14, "there" signifies not only "here" but "not here"—not present, therefore not visible to Barnardo who now asks this question nor to the audience who watches and listens to him speak. Similarly, the "piece" of Horatio he claims is "there" onstage implies the other piece or pieces of him that is or are "elsewhere"—offstage pieces, not present in the play.[22]

Barnardo's next line, "Welcome, Horatio. Welcome, good Marcellus" (20) is both fully present as an act of verbal hospitality and also suggests, as Coleridge noted, an absent, offstage physical space "elsewhere"—a negative space to the positive space of the stage—from which Horatio and Marcellus have now come.[23]

At the risk of trying my reader's patience further, let me go through the next lines more quickly, pointing to a couple of the more noticeable—and also, at least in the theater, unnoticed—instances where the play's language crosses the physical boundary of the stage. My point again is to demonstrate how much of *Hamlet* is concerned with offstage action, action we cannot see in the theater because it is not performed onstage except in words that invite us to imagine the reality of things beyond the reality of what we can see.

In line 21, Horatio's "What, has this thing appeared again tonight?" implies the continuation of a past during which "this thing" first made its appearance.[24] In Barnardo's "I have seen nothing" (22), we do not notice that we did not see Barnardo not see something. We also did not see or hear Horatio say "'tis but our fantasy" in line 23 (he said it prior to this moment, offstage and his speech is being reported by Marcellus), nor did we see Marcellus and Barnardo see "this dreaded sight twice seen of us" (25). Nor did we see or hear Marcellus "entreat . . . him [Horatio] along/ With us to watch the minute of this night" (26–27), a request he must again have made offstage sometime before the present moment. Marcellus's proposal in lines 28–29, "if this apparition come,/ He may approve our eyes," supposes that whatever may again appear will come from "elsewhere"—some place not visible either to the guards or to us—and that Horatio, in seeing it, will be able to confirm what we have not seen Marcellus and Barnardo see. Horatio's "Tush, tush, 'twill not appear" (30) projects a time in the future we will never see, since the Ghost is in fact about to appear. And Barnardo's "let us once again assail your ears,/ That are so fortified against our story,/ What we two nights have seen" (32–34) simultaneously projects a multitude of past events—actions we have not witnessed because they do not take place in the play: Barnardo's previous tellings of his story; Horatio's previous resistance to it; Barnardo's two sightings of the Ghost—plus one event (Barnardo's telling of his story) that will not take place because the Ghost's sudden appearance interrupts it. Finally, everything in that part of the story which Barnardo begins now to tell,

> Last night of all,
> When yond same star that's westward from the pole
> Had made his course t' illume that part of heaven
> Where now it burns, Marcellus and myself,
> The bell then beating one— (35–39)

refers to actions and events not performed onstage except in words, which, as Wittgenstein put it, "serve . . . as a picture" of unseen actions and events and "describe how things are." And then the crucial (unspoken, therefore unheard) stage direction, "Enter Ghost"—whose call for action brings to the stage the embodiment of everything that happens offstage in *Hamlet*: everything we cannot see since it is not performed onstage except in words (words, in whose "failure" to enact, literally to be, the actual physical things they refer to Shakespeare dramatizes the possibilities but also limits of theater itself, whose representation of dramatic physical and verbal actions is never quite what it seems, nor as real as its performance of those actions would have us believe).

I could obviously go on with such a reading of *Hamlet*, pointing out the presence of physically unperformed offstage action in the play—things we do not even notice we do not notice not taking place onstage, things we would experience in the theater in far less time than I have taken to describe them here. But to do so would cost me whatever readers have had the patience to bear with me thus far: no one wants to pay attention to what is missing from the thing one most wants to pay attention to—least of all from a play that has become "a universal cultural reference point, a piece of social shorthand."[25] And so I will end simply by saying that what is not performed physically in *Hamlet* is not missing from the performance of Hamlet, since everything I have pointed to in the opening lines of the play does in fact "appear" in words: those "Words, words, words" (2.2.192) that "show" us things we do not see, construct a picture of the world, describe how things are ("there") and how they might also be (here) imagined.

2

"My Sea Gown Scarfed About Me": Hamlet's Voyage to "Elsewhere"

I want to turn now to one example of offstage action in *Hamlet*—one that will let me continue to show how my approach works, why it matters and what can be learned about the play by thinking about the relation between the described reference and the language that produces it: Hamlet's voyage to "Elsewhere"—by which I mean not only England the island (which never appears in the play, upon whose shores Hamlet never lands) but everything that happens on the ship bound from Elsinore to England, action "performed" only in words. The performance of those events we do not "see" except in those words, which are both written (Hamlet's letters to Horatio and to Claudius announcing his return) and spoken (Hamlet's speech to Horatio telling him how he discovered Claudius's letter and forged a new one), "shows" us things that do not actually "happen" in the play, that is, are not performed physically in the play. Inviting us to see things that are not in front of us, Shakespeare asks us to imagine an "elsewhere" far from the world of Elsinore that is now being performed onstage. And in taking us, not in performed physical actions but words only, to that unseen place on the high seas, he also asks us to travel into our own minds, where we can "see" things that the "evidence" of Hamlet's written and spoken words "shows"—things we do not, as I say, actually see.

Hamlet's voyage to England has often been seen as a turning point in the play, after which Hamlet becomes "a changed man," as John Dover Wilson writes, apparently ready to do what he needs to do (and has not, up until this point, been able to do) in order to kill Claudius.[1] But how is it that the turning point of this most interior, claustrophobic of plays, which is staged almost entirely inside the walls of Elsinore—court chambers, closets, bedrooms, graves, with assorted references to mousetraps, nutshells, prison houses, vials, goblets, ears—takes place so far beyond the play's stage boundary, as far from Elsinore as this verbal voyage to "elsewhere"? And if the turning point of *Hamlet* takes place during Hamlet's voyage to England, which happens in words only, is the action of those performed verbal events the cause of its turn or simply the location, an unseen place of action we hear about but do not see (not eye- but earwitnessed) after which Hamlet is said to be "a changed man"? Finally, if Hamlet's return from the North Sea must be imagined in the words the play uses to perform it, where exactly has he returned from?

Not from England certainly, because Hamlet never actually arrives there in the play. Nor from the two ships sailing on the North Sea, the first heading for two days from Elsinore to England, the second heading in the opposite direction back to Elsinore, since those ships do not really exist, though the play wants us to believe that "Hamlet" (by which I mean the actor who plays him, who is waiting in the wings for Hamlet's return as "a changed man" in 5.1) has indeed been aboard each of those two ships. Rather, and obviously, the world that Hamlet returns from exists in words only—specifically, in the words Hamlet uses to describe it, whether in speaking or in writing.[2]

In taking an audience beyond the play's physical stage boundary, the world of offstage action represented by Hamlet's voyage to
England suggests several things at once, none of which are shown
in the play: London, where Shakespeare's audience first watched
the play and where "The present death of Hamlet" (4.3.64) was
to have taken place, had he ever arrived there; Hamlet's father's
orchard, where the Ghost says he was murdered when his brother
poured the "juice of cursed hebona" (1.5.62) in his ears; the afterlife, from which the Ghost has returned and which, were he to
describe it,

> Would harrow up thy soul, freeze thy young blood,
> Make thy two eyes like stars start from their spheres,
> Thy knotted and combinèd locks to part,
> And each particular hair to stand an end
> Like quills upon the fearful porcupine. (1.5.16–20)

Hamlet's "undiscovered country, from whose bourn / No traveler
returns" (3.1.79–80), which he imagines waits for us after death;
and the brook into which Ophelia falls or jumps—also water and
also not shown, another offstage site of death in *Hamlet*, death
performed in words only.[3]

Hamlet's physical return to the scene of the play in 5.1 comes
after his "reappearance" in the words of his two letters—the first
one to Horatio in 4.6, the second one to Claudius in 4.7.[4] The
letter to Horatio must have been given to the Sailor who gives
it to Horatio by Hamlet himself, whom the Sailor calls "th' am-
bassador that was bound for England" (4.6.10–11) and who must
therefore be standing on Danish soil instead of on the pirate ship,
presumably heading for Elsinore or waiting nearby to meet with
Horatio, who asks the Sailor to "direct me / To him from whom
you brought [these letters]" (32–33), that is to say, to somewhere
just offstage. When Horatio *"Reads the letter"* (sd 13) aloud, he im-
personates Hamlet, reading the words of Hamlet's disembodied

voice as if Hamlet were himself there, also present onstage, like Horatio, in front of us. The letter begins by addressing Horatio by his name ("Horatio"), as if Hamlet were there in person—a suggestion taken literally in Laurence Olivier's 1948 film *Hamlet*, in which the words are spoken not by Horatio but Hamlet himself (played by Olivier) who supposedly wrote them. Hamlet's spoken words in the film seem to have the power to recreate the events at sea described by those words: how the pirate ship overtakes the Danish one, how Hamlet leaps from one ship onto the other, how the pirate ship sails away. Here is the text of Hamlet's letter as read by Horatio (who "speaks" in Hamlet's voice) in Olivier's film:

" . . . Ere we were two days old at sea, a pirate of very warlike appoint-ment gave us chase. Finding ourselves too slow of sail, we put on a compelled valor, and in the grapple I boarded them. On the instant they got clear of our ship: so I alone became their prisoner. They have dealt with me like thieves of mercy, but they knew what they did: I am to do a good turn for them. . . . [R]epair thou to me with as much speed as thou wouldest fly death. . . . These good fellows will bring thee where I am. . . . Farewell. / He that thou knowest thine, Hamlet." (4.6.15–30)

In presenting this action on the screen, which is not performed onstage physically, only in the words that Horatio speaks in read-ing Hamlet's words, Olivier's film shows us pictures of action other than the action we see being performed in the play (Horatio stand-ing there speaking the words supposedly written by Hamlet). In Olivier's film Horatio does not actually read Hamlet's letter; his lips do not move, the voice we hear is not Norman Wooland's (the actor who plays him) but Olivier's, whose voice-over narra-tion accompanies, as the camera moves, a series of visual images: first a stone wall next to where Horatio stands; then a grey-white cloudlike mist coming in from the right across the stone wall (or is the wall turning into mist, or water?); then a pair of obviously toy boats on a miniature wave-tossed body of water, the pirate ship on a port tack heading in from the left, white sails billowing; then a close-up shot of the fight, Hamlet swinging down from the left on a rope, landing on the pirate deck wielding his sword; then a close-up of the sails; then a distant shot of the ships sailing away, one veering off to the left of the other; then a close-up of Hamlet and the pirates superimposed on an image of the two ships (the pirate in front appears to be the same sailor who handed Horatio the letter); and finally the pirate ship fading into the mist again, which itself fades to a close-up of Horatio standing in front of the stone wall, listening at this point to the end of a speech by Hamlet himself, who, in the play at least, is not there except in his words.

"Performing" what an audience sitting at the play *Hamlet* does not actually see, Olivier's film shows us what the play represents in words only—two ships at sea, men "grappling," Hamlet jumping from one ship to another before the second ship sails away. And in thus showing what is not seen in the theater (can't be performed "realistically"), it also compresses action that must have taken many minutes, even hours, to occur into a few quick visual scenes—a visual narrative of what Hamlet's language pictures in a few short lines of prose. At the same time, it overlooks things that Shakespeare thought important enough to put into the play: Hamlet's instructions to Horatio ("when thou shalt have overlooked this, give these men some means to the king" [13–16], and "Let the king have the letters I have sent" [22–23]); his promise of things to come ("I have words to speak in thine ear will make thee dumb, yet are they much too light for the bore of the matter. These good fellows will bring thee to where I am. Rosencrantz and Guildenstern hold their course for England. Of them I have much to tell thee" [24–29]), which will come up later, when Hamlet tells Horatio what else happened while he was at sea.[5]

Following his "appearance" in the words of his letters to

Horatio and Claudius, Hamlet's physical return to the stage of *Hamlet* provides further verbal evidence of the offstage action that took place aboard the ship bound from Denmark to England. But unlike those two letters, what he says to Horatio in person focuses not on the public "grapple" between men on ships but the private reading and writing of letters that preceded it:

> Up from my cabin,
> My sea gown scarfed about me, in the dark
> Groped I to find out them, had my desire,
> Fingered their packet, and in fine withdrew
> To mine own room again, making so bold,
> My fears forgetting manners, to unseal
> Their grand commission; where I found, Horatio—
> Ah, royal knavery!—an exact command,
> Larded with many several sorts of reasons,
> Importing Denmark's health, and England's too,
> With, ho! such bugs and goblins in my life,
> That on the supervise, no leisure bated,
> No, not to stay the grinding of the ax,
> My head should be struck off. (5.2.12–25)

At which point Horatio interrupts him ("Is't possible"), Hamlet giving him "the commission" as physical proof before he goes on to say how he forged a new letter—"[a]n earnest conjuration from the king" (38)—ordering that "[h]e should those bearers put to sudden death" (46), stamped it with his "father's signet . . . the model of that Danish seal" (49–50), then "[s]ubscribed" and "placed" this new letter "safely, / The changeling never known" (52–53). And so it is that "Rosencrantz and Guildenstern go to't" (56), as Horatio says to Hamlet, another instance of offstage death—like Hamlet's father's, like Ophelia's—one we are asked to imagine from the words the play uses to "perform" it, since it is not shown physically (and thus not seen) in the play.

  I want to go back to Hamlet's fourteen-line speech to Horatio (sonnet-like in length, but like no sonnet Shakespeare ever wrote) telling him how he found the letter that Rosencrantz and Guildenstern were delivering from Claudius to the king of England and what it said, to demonstrate how its words work to "perform" what they refer to—offstage action that is not performed physically in the play but only in these words, which *Hamlet's* critics have for the most part ignored, maybe because this speech comes immediately after a speech that seems to be so much more important, the one that appears to explain the new Hamlet ("a changed man" it seems, since his "sudden and more strange return" from England):

> Rashly,
> And praised be rashness for it—let us know,
> Our indiscretion sometime serves us well
> When our deep plots do pall, and that should learn us
> There's a divinity that shapes our ends
> Rough-hew them how we will. (5.2.6–11)

As I have noted, critics have pointed to the idea of "divinity" in this speech to explain Hamlet's apparently changed behavior after he returns from England. But the things I want to talk about in Hamlet's "Up from my cabin" speech have not, as far as I know, been talked about by anyone, not because they are not important to the play—quite the contrary, the things I am going to talk about here (things embedded in the play's language that we hear but do not notice, things that conceal what Harry Berger, Jr. has called "surplus meaning"[6]) are what makes *Hamlet* so wonderful—but because they call almost no attention to themselves: so little attention that a theater audience is unlikely to notice any of these things while watching and listening to the play in performance, so little attention that even critics who have thought about *Hamlet* primarily as a play-text have overlooked them. So I want to make it clear that in thinking about the things I am going to focus on here,

which will take me far longer to talk about than it will take the actor playing Hamlet to deliver these lines, I realize that no one at
a performance of *Hamlet* is likely to notice (consciously, at least)
these things, and that is the point: things we do not notice when
hearing the play performed (which are in the play even though
we do not hear them) are like the things we also do not see—the
offstage action that is not performed physically in the play, only in
words (these words in fact) which dramatize the offstage, imagined
action they describe and invite us to see.

Unlike his father who was murdered in his orchard while he
slept, Hamlet seems to have escaped Claudius's plot against his
life (which will unfold in England) because, as he tells Horatio,
"in my heart there was a kind of fighting / That would not let me
sleep" (5.2.4–5). The five syllables missing from the end of line
12 ("Up from my cabin") give the adverb's direction a moment
of time in which a verb's action (still missing at this point) can
take place. Since it presents only direction ("Up") and location
from which ("my cabin"), Hamlet's first line in this speech seems
to project action itself, outward or rather upward from the con-
fined space of a "cabin" on a ship[7]—it recalls both Ophelia's closet,
which Hamlet had once visited while she was sewing there, and
his mother's bedroom—whose sleepless inhabitant has suddenly
("rashly") been launched, why and toward what we do not know.
As such, giving us only the result of an as yet missing action by an
also as yet missing subject, line 12 "performs" in words the new
"changed" Hamlet—now, since his return from England but as
this line makes clear starting while he was gone, a man of unadul-
terated action, a man who no longer has to look (or think) before
he leaps, who can jump without a moment's notice into a grave or
even up from a cabin.

Thus begun by launching its disembodied, still absent speaker
upward, Hamlet's speech moves forward in the next line by shift-

ing attention from action to what the actor wears: "My sea gown scarfed about me, in the dark." "My sea gown," which repeats the possessive construction of "my cabin" and also something of its idea (they both enclose), recalls other items of Hamlet's clothing in the play: his "inky cloak" and "customary suits of solemn black" (1.2.77–78), his "doublet all unbraced," "stockings fouled, / Ungartered, and down-gyvèd to his ankle" and "[p] ale . . . shirt" (2.1.77–80). But if clothes do indeed make the man, the man wearing this "sea gown" seems to be quite different indeed from the one whose "suspiration of forced breath," "fruitful river in the eye" and "dejected havior of the visage" (1.2.79–81) first appeared in the play, the one whose knees were "knocking each other" (2.2.80) in Ophelia's closet. Someone more like Errol Flynn or Johnny Depp it seems, swashbuckler with "sea gown" (it must be green—but "in the dark" who can tell) "scarfed about" him, close-up camera working to show us what we cannot see (it is offstage, and also "in the dark"; someone as dashing, literally charming as the line's interlocking pairs of sounds: long *e* in "sea" and "me" surrounding *ou* of "gown" and "about," *ar* of "scarfed" echoed in "dark."

Thus clothed in his dashing "sea gown" ("scarfed" acting like both verb and part of what he is wearing[8]), the action-hero moves upward "in the dark"—it is as if Hamlet has become a pirate even before the pirate ship comes to him, the treasures he looks for not gold and silver but a letter from the Danish king ordering his head "should be stuck off." Whereas "in the dark" at the end of line 13 seems at first (momentarily at least) to go with Hamlet's "sea gown scarfed," it proves in the following line (line 3 of this erstwhile sonnet: "Groped I to find out them, had my desire") to show us why Hamlet's sentence's subject "Groped": he could not see in the dark, needed to use his hands as eyes to feel his way out of "[his] cabin," through the ship's passageways, until he came to the place where he "found out them"—all of which must have taken some time it seems, much longer than it takes Hamlet to tell Horatio what happened when "Groped I to find out them." The vaguely sexual feeling of "groped" suggested here, which lies somewhere below the surface and is in part what makes this speech about off-stage action so strange, so sonnetlike perhaps but also so perfor-mative of the change that seems to have come over Hamlet—the man of action who, as he tells Horatio, "had [his] desire, / Fingered their packet, and in fine withdrew"—is further continued as the sentence (which will not end until this speech concludes) un-folds.[9] In pointing out the possibility of sexual innuendo in these two lines, I do not mean to suggest anything other than the pos-sibility that these meanings may lie somewhere below the surface of what the lines clearly say and are understood to say: Hamlet found his way through the dark to a room where Rosencrantz and Guildenstern (still unnamed at this point) were evidently asleep, took "their packet," then went back to his own room. At the same time, the play of possible sexual meanings in this context resonates back and forth throughout the play.[10]

All of the action described in Hamlet's speech up to this point must have taken how long—five minutes perhaps, perhaps ten or even fifteen?—how long would it have taken Hamlet to find his way along the passageways of the ship, find Rosencrantz and Guildenstern's room, find and then "Finger . . . their packet," find his way back "to [his] own room again"? Surely much longer than these few lines in Hamlet's speech to Horatio has taken to de-scribe these actions (perhaps fifteen seconds to deliver these five and a half lines—which deal with what happens between the time Hamlet leaves his "cabin" to the time he gets back to his "own room again"), which may well have been Shakespeare's reason for making Hamlet's voyage to England happen offstage, action spo-ken in words only, an already long play otherwise growing longer

than his audience would have stood for. But also, and nonetheless compelling from the dramatist's point of view, how could an
actor—even the leading actor in Shakespeare's company—show
us those physical actions that Hamlet's words "show," inviting us
to see and imagine things (in our mind's eye) that no actor playing Hamlet will be able to perform, not because he is not skilled
enough but because no physical gesture can suggest what words
like "My sea gown scarfed about me, in the dark/ Groped I . . . had
my desire, / Fingered their packet" suggest. That is to say, words
like "Fingered their packet" enable us to "see" something beyond the actions being performed physically onstage (by actors
pretending they are characters speaking these words), something
"elsewhere"—as imagined and imaginary as the play itself is.

What we "see" in line 16 when Hamlet returns "To mine own
room again, making so bold" echoes things we have heard in previous lines—the idea of "cabin" in "room," possessive construction of "my cabin," "My sea-gown," and "my desire" in "mine own
room" (which is itself echoed in "My fears," "my life" and, ultimately, "My head" below), sounds of "fine" in "mine," "withdrew"
in "room," "groped" in both "own" and "so bold"—things we do
not notice in the theater of course but nonetheless have heard,
subliminally perhaps, sound effects calling little (or no) attention
to themselves perhaps being part of the reason why critics have
overlooked this speech, understandably enough when lines like
"Our indiscretion sometime serves us well" and "There's a divinity that shapes our ends,/Rough-hew them how we will" are so
much more important to the meaning of the play, it seems. On
the contrary, the unobtrusive (therefore unnoticed) patterns of
sounds that I point to here "perform" Shakespeare's "big ideas" in
Hamlet—ideas like "indiscretion" and "shapes" and "Rough-hew"
for instance (not to forget "divinity," which somehow gives meaning to "our ends") which are literally sounded, demonstrated in

the surface of the play's words, so that language itself is enacting what Shakespeare was thinking (also thinking about) when he wrote these words.

This is not to say that we can "get back" to what Shakespeare "meant" when he wrote *Hamlet*, no "evidence" of that except the play's words (several "authentic" printed versions)—no manuscript or working drafts or Boswell to record what Shakespeare said in the tavern after a day's work. And so in this speech the work must have been to get to what Hamlet discovered when he opened then read the letter as quickly as possible, fourteen lines perhaps a coincidence but as good a length (given the urgency of the matter at hand, both Hamlet's need to tell Horatio what he "found" in the letter and Shakespeare's need to speed the play's action forward to its end) as any. The sounds of the words getting to the news at the end of the speech ("My head should be struck off") were—and still are—things, simply part of the physical "packet," as Hamlet puts it, by which I mean to suggest that the letter he opens in this scene has an uncanny similarity to the play in which he opens and reads that letter, its missing words recalled now when Hamlet finally gets around to telling his friend what it said ("My head should be struck off"). So even though the speech is fairly short at least by Hamlet's standards (only fourteen lines; compare the "To be or not to be" speech's 33 lines, the "O, what a rogue and peasant slave am I" speech's 56 lines), it still takes its time in getting to what it gets to, still conveys the substance of its action in the shaped sounds of words that only seem and sound rough-hewn, the discreteness of whose many patterns (of sounds and also sense) may well not be noticed by any listener watching the play in the theater, their "indiscretion" serving to connect disparate elements in the surface of the play's text to each other across the spaces that also divide them (sound connected to sound and word meaning to word meaning, the grammar of this idea connected to that one), a great deal of which goes in one ear and out the other when we watch and listen to the play being performed in the theater. Anyone who doubts the validity of what I say here need only recall what it was like to hear (and see) Hamlet telling Horatio what happened on the ship bound for England. We do not have time to notice let alone think about any of what I have been noticing and thinking about here because it all goes by too quickly, because the spell cast by the actor who plays this part overwhelms whatever attention we might, in the privacy of our own armchairs, otherwise give to these words. Which is as it should be, since the play was written to be performed onstage in the theater rather than read on the page, my reading of its words clearly a violation of its physically sensuous appeal as a staged, theatrical event.

What Hamlet "shows" us as his speech races to its last line might well seem less picturesque than its beginning—no "sea gowns scarfed" or groping in the dark, no fingering of "their packet." Instead we get something more interior, less physical and therefore not so easily seen—the courage Hamlet summons up in "making so bold," "fears forgetting manners," a "grand commission," "royal knavery," "many several sorts of reasons," "Denmark's health, and England's too," "my life," "supervise, no leisure bated,/No, not to stay the grinding of the ax"—at which we are shocked back to the concrete "reality" of the situation Hamlet's words are trying (and also failing) to represent. Nothing that he says onstage here will make what happened offstage there ("elsewhere") present again or visible to us who are hearing him speak these words. Likewise no gesture that an actor might make onstage could show us what Hamlet's "making so bold,/My fears forgetting manners" shows us of his interior—invisible, unseeable—condition, nor could a physical gesture "echo" what the word "forgetting" recalls: "Remember me" (1.5.91), "the table of my memory" (1.5.98), "If it live in your memory, begin at this line" (2.2.388–89).[11] While

Hamlet's "forgetting" his good "manners" enables him to unseal a letter addressed we assume to the king of England, what he is doing in telling Horatio about it is not forgetting but recalling what took place offstage ("elsewhere," "in the past"): the memory that his words "perform" onstage—interior and invisible until put into words—is conveyed to Horatio (and to us) in the words he uses to remember it, is "materialized" in words that, while they will not make what happened aboard the ship physically present on the stage (will inevitably "fail" to reproduce those events that happened "elsewhere," that are still alive in Hamlet's memory), will nevertheless "show" us and enable us to "see" what no physical gesture can ever show (because it is inside, cannot be seen).

And so, unable to show or make present what happened offstage but still able to perform it verbally, in ways that "show" us more than any physical gesture can, Hamlet's speech speeds headlong forward to an end in which he finally reveals Claudius's letter's "exact command": that his "head should be struck off." Had I world enough and time, I could continue to think about how the words in the speech work to "perform" the imagined action it talks about—noting things like the oxymoronic pairing of "royal knavery," which echoes what Hamlet has previously called both Claudius, who is responsible for this example of "royal knavery" ("There's never a villain dwelling in all Denmark / But he's an arrant knave" [1.5.123–24]) and all other men as well (who as he says to Ophelia "are arrant knaves all" [3.1.129]), including Polonius "Who was in life a foolish prating knave" (3.4.215) and the Gravedigger ("How absolute the knave is! We must speak by the card" [5.1.128–29]), not to mention his "knavish piece of work" (3.2.236) in *The Mousetrap*. Noting also the echo in "exact command" of Hamlet asking the Ghost in the closet scene if he comes "your tardy son to chide" for failing to execute "your dread command" (3.4.106–8), a line that links these two brothers as commanding fathers to Polonius, who as Ophelia tells him "did command [that she] did repel his letters" (2.1.107–8). I would also point to the various, complexly related echoes in "Larded with many several sorts of reasons" not only of Ophelia's "Larded all with sweet flowers" (4.5.38) and "that noble and most sovereign reason / Like sweet bells jangled" (3.1.157–58) but Hamlet's "pales and forts of reason" (1.4.28), "how noble in reason" (2.2.273–74) and "reason panders will" (3.4.88), Claudius's "two special reasons" (4.7.9), and Gertrude's "He's fat, and scant of breath" (5.2.270). And the similarly complexly-related echoes (also similarly unnoticed in the theater) in "Importing Denmark's health" of Hamlet's question to the Ghost, "Be thou a spirit of health or goblin damned" (1.4.40), which is echoed in the following line by "goblins"—demons that suggest the play's ghost, Claudius's "Importing health and graveness" (4.7.79) and "Here's to thy health" (5.2.266), and many references to disease beginning with Francisco being "sick at heart" (1.1.9) and including Marcellus's "Something is rotten in the state of Denmark" (1.4.90)—"Denmark" appears twenty-two times in *Hamlet* and nowhere else in Shakespeare—and Gertrude's "my sick soul" (4.5.17). And also the various (and unnoticed) echoes in "such bugs" of paired short *u* sounds in "Up from" at the beginning of this speech and paired ideas in "No, not" in the next line of this speech and of the many animals in the play beginning with Francisco's "Not a mouse stirring" (1.1.10) and including Hamlet's and Polonius's exchange about whether "yonder cloud" looks like a camel, a weasel, or "Very like a whale" (3.2.369–75). And also the echoes in "leisure"—also not noticed in the theater— of Polonius telling Ophelia not to "slander any moment leisure" (1.3.132) by talking to Hamlet and Hamlet telling Horatio to read Claudius's "commission . . . at more leisure" (5.2.26), followed by Osric telling Hamlet that if he "were at leisure" (5.2.76-77) he would "impart" a message to him from Claudius. And the echoes in "bated"—again not noticed by anyone watching the play—of Claudius saying to Laertes that he "may choose / A sword unbated" (4.7.135–36) followed by Laertes telling Claudius "I'll annoint my sword" and "touch my point / With this contagion" (138, 144–45). And, last but not least, an echo—most certainly not noticed in the theater—in "grinding of the ax" of Horatio remembering how Hamlet's father "smote the sledded Polacks on the ice" (1.1.63)— an echo both of sound and the idea of striking with a blade, which the last line of Hamlet's speech to Horatio finally delivers: "My head should be struck off." But I have already said enough (if not too much) about this speech.

And so I will end this chapter by saying once again that everything I have noticed in the preceding paragraph will not be noticed by anyone watching and listening to a performance of the play in the theater. What we see when we watch Hamlet telling Horatio about things we do not see—what happened offstage on the ship bound for England—is Hamlet talking to Horatio. What we do not see are the actions he describes, just as what we do not hear (or notice in the theater, at least) in his words is how they "echo"— connect to, play with or against—other words in lines elsewhere in the play. In watching and listening to the play performed in the theater, we are aware that we are not getting all of it, that we must see it again, or go home to read it again. This is why *Hamlet* has continued to exert such power over its audiences for all of these years—we know there is more to it than meets the eye, and ear too for that matter.

3

"Counterfeit Presentment": The Ghost's Speech

Having thought about the opening lines of the play, breaking off just at the entrance of the Ghost (a physical embodiment of everything that takes place offstage in *Hamlet*, everything we cannot see, everything we only hear about in words), I want now to think about the Ghost's speech on his own death—the murder of the person he was, the murder of King Hamlet.[1] And in taking up this particular passage from *Hamlet*—words that "remember" action that happens before the play begins; action that is itself "remembered" two more times in the play, one in gestures only (the dumb show) and one in words-plus-gestures (*The Mousetrap* play)—I want to think about how the words of this speech, which themselves gesture at the impossibility of representation, the inability of words to enact physical things, both "perform" the world of the play but also fail to show us what is not physically present in that world—call it the unseeable, unknowable, unrepresentable. Here, then, is the Ghost's speech:

> Brief let me be. Sleeping within my orchard,
> My custom always of the afternoon,
> Upon my secure hour thy uncle stole
> With juice of cursed hebona in a vial,

And in the porches of my ears did pour
The leperous distillment, whose effect
Holds such an enmity with blood of man
That swift as quicksilver it courses through
The natural gates and alleys of the body
And with a sudden vigor it doth posset
And curd, like eager droppings into milk,
The thin and wholesome blood. So did it mine,
And a most instant tetter barked about
Most lazarlike with vile and loathsome crust
All my smooth body. (1.5.59–73)

In the reading that follows I will talk in detail about how a death that is not performed physically in *Hamlet* happens in the words *Hamlet* uses to "perform" it—words that are, as Hamlet says, a "counterfeit presentment" (3.4.54) of action that does not actually happen in *Hamlet*, a "forgèd process of . . . death," as the Ghost says (1.5.37). Focusing on the presence of a multitude of casual, apparently insignificant patterns of verbal interaction whose presence will not be noticed by an audience in the theater, I will argue what is obvious—that Claudius does not kill his brother *in* the play; that this speech imagines a world beyond the world of the stage, a world made of words in which the eye sees only what the ear hears, thus sounding the limits of perception itself; that the play's three-part representation of King Hamlet's death—once in words without action (the Ghost's speech), once in actions-without-words (the dumb show), once in words-plus-actions (the play within the play)—presents Shakespeare's most profound articulation of theatrical language, a language of gestures and words, whose physics may be further understood in terms of what Stanley Cavell has called "the relation or argument in the theater between the eye and the ear, representation by action and by words, showing and saying."[2]

Before turning to the speech, let me point out what is obvious:

the person who speaks these lines onstage is missing—is not King Hamlet but his Ghost, is not a ghost but an actor playing a ghost. King Hamlet, whose body does not appear in the play (though he is present in the body of an actor who plays the part of the incorporeal Ghost), may be understood to stand for everything missing from the play—action that does not appear because it happens offstage (words only) and, on another level, in the reader's experience of the play as words on the page, *everything* in the play, all of its action, which must be imagined from the words that the play's characters speak. That is to say, as the embodied spirit of King Hamlet, the Ghost stands for what is *not shown* on the stage of *Hamlet*, whose words in the Ghost's speech also "show" us the interior of the king's body—which cannot be seen or even performed—even as we take them up, project them onto the screens of our imagination, where they may be "read" as a theater of the text whose "actors"—words—"perform" the events they invite us to imagine, witness, "see."[3]

How are we to understand this death of King Hamlet, that missing action from which all the action in *Hamlet* follows? Which leads me also to ask, how is death itself dramatized in the play? It is embodied, first of all, in the character named "Ghost of Hamlet's Father," the last person listed in the Folio's Names of the Actors, identified not by name but by his role in a play that imagines, as it is performed onstage, what happens when that son is visited by that father—or that father returns to haunt that son. And, as an event that has taken place before the time of the play, it is also performed verbally, in the Ghost's account of how his brother murdered him. That same death is also (I am moving now chronologically through the play, counting only what I should call its major deaths) performed twice again in the play's ninth scene, first in theatrical pantomime:

Enter a King and a Queen [very lovingly], the Queen embracing him, and he her. [She kneels; and makes show of protestation unto him.] He takes her up, and declines his head upon her neck. He lies him down upon a bank of flowers. She, seeing him asleep, leaves him. Anon come in another man: takes off his crown, kisses it, pours poison in the sleeper's ears, and leaves him. The Queen returns, finds the King dead, makes passionate action. The poisoner, with some three or four, come in again, seem to condole with her. The dead body is carried away. The poisoner woos the Queen with gifts; she seems harsh awhile, but in the end accepts love;

and then in the performance of *The Mousetrap*, "the image of a murder done in Vienna" as Hamlet says (3.2.234), where it is not actually performed, since Claudius breaks off that play within the play before it gets to the act that Hamlet has promised it will perform.

Other deaths, accomplished by other means, are performed on-stage when Hamlet stabs Polonius through the arras, and in the play's final scene when Gertrude drinks from the poisoned cup, Laertes stabs Hamlet with the poisoned sword, Hamlet stabs Laertes with that same sword, then uses it on Claudius whom he finishes off by forcing him to "Drink off" the cup's last drops of poison. Still other deaths are not actually performed onstage except in words—words that "show" us things the play performs only in words, which the play's actors pour into the ears of its audience: Ophelia's death by drowning; the death of Fortinbras-the-father in combat with King Hamlet, an event that took place thirty years before the time of the events unfolding on the stage of *Hamlet*; the deaths of "fathers, mothers, daughters, sons" at the hand of "[t]he rugged Pyrrhus, he whose sable arms, / Black as his purpose, did the night resemble" (2.2.398, 392–93), whose "bleeding sword" (431) goes on in the Player's speech to slaughter helpless Priam; the death of Julius Caesar enacted by Polonius ("I was killed i' th' Capitol; Brutus killed me" (3.2.101–2); "the imminent death," in Hamlet's words, "of twenty thousand men / That for a fantasy and trick of fame / Go to their graves like beds" (4.4.60–62); the death of the man in Ophelia's mad song, who "will a not come again? / And will a not come again" (4.5.184–85); the death of men implicit in the flowers that "cold maids [call] dead-men's-fingers" (4.7.169); death again personified in the Frenchman whom Laertes calls Lamord ("la mort"); the hypothetical death of the man in the gravedigger's speech, who, if he "go to this water and drown himself, it is, will he nill he, he goes. . . . But if the water come to him and drown him, he drowns not himself" (5.1.15–18); the deaths of those several men whose skulls the gravedigger "throws up" from the hole in the ground he digs for Ophelia—the skull that "had a tongue in it, and could sing once" (5.1.70–71), perhaps a "politician" or courtier; the skull that may have belonged to a lawyer, and the one identified by the gravedigger (the play's forensic expert) as "Yorick's . . . the king's jester" (5.1.170); the death of the man who, according to the gravedigger, will lie in the ground "some eight or nine year. A tanner will last you nine year" (5.1.156–57); the death of Alexander who, once "buried . . . returneth to dust" (5.1.198–99) and (once again) Caesar, "dead and turned to clay (202); the "sudden death" of Rosencrantz and Guildenstern, who, once arrived in England, supposedly "go to't" (5.2.56) without a second thought; this whole parade of deaths leading in conclusion to "this fell sergeant, Death," (5.2.319) whom Hamlet invokes before "The potent poison quite o'ercrows [his] spirit" (336), sending him to a "rest" that is indeed "silence."[4]

Five of the deaths in *Hamlet* are caused by poison, ingested first (before the play begins) as a "leperous distillment" poured into King Hamlet's two "ears"; then as "the drink, the drink!" (5.2.292) Gertrude swallows—knowingly or not? we do not know—and Claudius is soon thereafter made to swallow; and then, in the suddenly rushing final moments of a play whose course of action has seemed prior to this point to drag, slow, twist and bend, as the "instrument . . . envenomed" (5.2.299–300) that pierces the skin first of Hamlet and Laertes (who, the Folio stage direction seems to imply, receive their fatal wounds at almost the same frantic moment: *"In scuffling they change rapiers"*) and then of Claudius whose life his nephew/stepson has been meaning to take from him since the fifth scene of the play.[5] All but one of these deaths takes place physically onstage, in full view both of the characters who are present onstage in the play's final scene—the two sons, Hamlet and Laertes; Claudius and Gertrude (who dies before she witnesses the deaths of those who will soon follow her); Horatio, Osric and whoever else may be implied by the generic "ALL" (who cry "Treason! treason!" when Hamlet stabs Claudius [306])—and also of us in the audience, who witness, as these characters do, everything taking place in the present action being performed onstage.

The one death that is not performed onstage physically—the one represented in the Ghost's story of what happened a month or so before the play begins—is the only one that performs in detail what happens when poison enters the body. That is to say, in every other physical death in *Hamlet* what we see with our eyes is all we get; in the death of Hamlet's father, however, which we do not see performed physically onstage but are asked to imagine in the words the Ghost uses to describe it, what we hear in words takes us *inside* of the king's body—well beyond that "rest" that is "silence," those stage boundaries beyond which we cannot see.

Like Hamlet's imagined vision of his mother and Claudius having sex "In the rank sweat of an enseamèd bed, / Stewed in corruption, honeying and making love / Over the nasty sty—" (3.4.92–94), which presents a mental picture of something that is performed verbally but not physically in the play, the Ghost's recounting of his murder by his brother imagines a theatrical space in which the eye "sees" only what the ear hears. Not only is the scene of Hamlet's father's murder not performed physically onstage, it is "performed" by means of words whose effect is to "show" us what cannot be shown, penetrating King Hamlet's body (the "real stage" of the play) as they described the entrance of poison into that body, as if those words were themselves taking his life, which in a sense they are, since his death takes place in, and only by means of, words—is literally a death in language. The deaths we *see* being performed onstage—Polonius being stabbed through the arras, Hamlet and Laertes and Claudius being stabbed with the poisoned sword, Gertrude and then Claudius drinking from the poisoned cup—take place in the distance so to speak; we see in each instance an actor staging an imitation of death, a fake death, one caused by the supposed entrance of a foreign substance into the body whose exterior form (what we see) thereupon goes limp, collapses, falls to the stage. We know that in each case the body is not actually dead; that it will get up again, walk around and talk, go off to wherever that actor goes when the play is over: Polonius, whom Hamlet drags offstage still "dead," gets up offstage; Hamlet, Laertes, Claudius and Gertrude must stand up onstage, in full view of the audience—in the Globe at least, where there was no curtain to separate the world of the play from the world of the theater—who, applauding at the end of their performance, will seem to raise them from the dead. (Although we have been sitting offstage throughout the play, the sound called for by Fortinbras's command at the end of the play that military honors be paid to the dead Hamlet—"Go, bid the soldiers shoot" [5.2.386]—leads directly to the sound of our applause, thus making us as audience into actors whose role becomes not to honor the recent dead by shooting guns but to [re]call them to a life they never actually left by clapping our hands, thereby, as Prospero says in *The Tempest*, releasing them from the stage on which no real deaths have occurred.[6]) The death-by-poison we only hear about, however, a death performed only in the Ghost's words (then twice again, first in the dumb show, a physical counterpart to the Ghost's speech, then in *The Mousetrap* play's representation of that death in words-plus-actions), takes place directly in front of us, in the foreground so to speak of our imaginations.

Whereas the characters who are killed (or in Gertrude's case kill themselves) onstage come back to life only after the play is finished, Hamlet's father, who dies before the play begins, not only comes back to life before the play begins (he has been "twice seen" by the three sentinels prior to the time of the play) but appears during the play. Eyewitness to his own death, his dramatic purpose for Shakespeare—who may himself have played the part—is to tell Hamlet (and us) what happened while he was sleeping in the orchard, a scene that neither Hamlet nor *Hamlet*'s audience have witnessed. Thus, when he says how he was "by a brother's hand / Of life, of crown, of queen at once dispatched" (1.5.74–75), what enters Hamlet's (and *Hamlet*'s audience's) ears are the sounds of words describing the entrance of poison through the ear into the body. All of which suggests that this manner of death-by-poison-poured-into-ear followed by this ear/eyewitness account of that death are significant, especially in a play that pays as much attention to ears and speaking and listening as *Hamlet* does.[7]

I now want to look more closely at *Hamlet* 1.5.59–73, an amazingly convoluted speech in which the Ghost, having denounced his brother ("that incestuous, that adulterate beast") and wife ("my most seeming-virtuous queen") describes in detail his own death. Here again are those lines:

> Brief let me be. Sleeping within my orchard,
> My custom always of the afternoon,
> Upon my secure hour thy uncle stole

With juice of cursed hebona in a vial,
And in the porches of my ears did pour
The leperous distillment, whose effect
Holds such an enmity with blood of man
That swift as quicksilver it courses through
The natural gates and alleys of the body,
And with a sudden vigor it doth posset
And curd, like eager droppings into milk,
The thin and wholesome blood. So did it mine,
And a most instant tetter barked about
Most lazarlike with vile and loathsome crust
All my smooth body.

The speech is indeed labyrinthine, but its maze of parts—which we are likely not to notice in a performance of this speech by an actor—imagines a world that, though it is not performed physically onstage, is completely clear and understandable: as audience and readers, we understand from these words that Hamlet's father was murdered by his brother. At the same time, the capacity of these words to "perform" the action they refer to in words that nonetheless also fail to give real evidence (Othello's "ocular proof" [3.3.360]) of what happened in the orchard is what has made *Hamlet* so fascinating to audiences for more than four hundred years. The point is that we *must* speculate about things we cannot know because we do not ever see them: there is an emptiness, a hollow place filled by words that refer to actions that are not themselves there; hence mystery, doubt, uncertainty, unseeableness, unknowableness, non-presence of actual "real" phenomena; and so also the fact that we do not notice (in the theater at least) the verbal phenomena that I am going to talk about in the following pages—these things we hear (perhaps subliminally, although we do not consciously notice them) themselves being *like* actions performed offstage (whose physical "evidence" is missing from the play, cannot be seen and thus known because it exists only in words), actions we likewise do not see.

The speech begins—I should say continues, the Ghost has been speaking without interruption for seventeen lines—with a four-word sentence, "Brief let me be," which is both true and false, since this *is* the shortest sentence (by far) in a forty-nine-line speech that is also anything but "brief." Although "brief" in this context functions primarily as an adjective, meaning of short duration,[8] its substantive meanings (something written—a letter, note, statement, account, list, memorandum) work to suggest the metatheatrical nature of a speech in which this living actor, impersonating the Ghost of a man who has never lived, gives a long-winded, narrative, and indeed fictional account of the circumstances in which he died.

The long *e* sound in "Sleeping" at the start of the next sentence, which begins in line 59 and runs to the middle of line 70, connects it to the previous sentence not only phonetically (we hear long *e* in four of the line's first five syllables: *"Brief* let *me* be. *Slee*ping") but also substantively, since the Ghost has come to Hamlet because he wants to sleep but cannot, being instead "Doomed for a certain term to walk the night . . . Till the foul crimes done in my days of nature / Are burnt and purged away" (1.5.10–12).

A fleeting, accidental sense of the Ghost being unable to sleep but wanting to ("let me . . . Sleep") gives way, as the line continues, to a sense that he is "sleeping"—not as we might expect in bed but in an "orchard," a word that, derived from *hortus*, suggests not only a generic enclosed space for the cultivation of herbs and fruit trees but the garden of Eden, a sense suggested more directly in the Ghost's previous speech, the only other time that "orchard" appears in *Hamlet*, where he tells Hamlet something he must already know: "'Tis given out that, sleeping in my orchard, / A serpent stung me" (35–36). (It is curious, but also remarkably insignificant, that the link between trees in the orchard and King Hamlet's offstage death is echoed later in *Hamlet* by a connection between a willow tree by the river bank and Ophelia's offstage death.)

The transformation of a serpent in the orchard of that previous speech into Claudius ("The serpent that did sting thy father's life / Now wears his crown" [39–40]) is incidentally repeated in the opening words of the next line, which appear to stand in opposition to "my orchard, / My custom." But whereas "orchard" referred to the physical location of the king's nap, "custom" refers here to the act of napping itself—to King Hamlet's habit of napping "always of the afternoon," neither place nor the physical act taking place there performed onstage in *Hamlet* except in these words. Being thus invisible to the audience of *Hamlet* as well as to the reader of the text, King Hamlet asleep in his orchard becomes a "figment" of multiple imaginations: Shakespeare's, the Ghost's, Hamlet's, the actors' who play them, ours.

The pattern of grammatically and thematically linked possessives begun with "my orchard / My custom" continues with a twofold variation in the next line, "Upon my secure hour thy uncle stole." Whereas two previous possessive adjectives ("my" and "My") had been followed by nouns signifying first a place, then the action taking place there, this first possessive in line 61 is followed by an adjective-plus-noun combination ("my secure hour") signifying not place or act but the time of that act in that place. The time suggested in "hour" reiterates, but collapses the scope of, the time of "afternoon" in the preceding line, and the condition of that time suggested by "secure"[9] amplifies several ideas inherent in the words "custom" and "sleeping" in the two preceding lines: when one is asleep, one is free from care in one's habits.

The string of three first-person possessive pronoun-plus-noun combinations in "my orchard," "My custom," and "my . . . hour" is broken but also continued in the words "thy uncle stole" at the end of line 61, which in shifting from first to second person possessive directs our attention from the speaker to his auditor, Ghost to Hamlet, who thus appears to be implicated in the murder the Ghost's words are about to reenact. Which is to say, if Shakespeare had written, plausibly enough, "my brother" instead of "thy uncle," Hamlet could have remained merely a witness to what is about to take place; being explicitly identified as a blood relative of the person who, the Ghost claims, murdered him, on the other hand, makes Hamlet an accomplice to that murder, as if he too were now being accused of the crime his father's Ghost has begun to recount.

The shift from first to second person pronoun in "my . . . My . . . my . . . thy" resonates with the shift in syntax by means of which King Hamlet, who, according to the Ghost's account, has been sleeping in his orchard, becomes the uncle who "stole / With juice of cursed hebona in a vial." The grammatical stealth of a sentence that slips from one subject to another (the father who slept to uncle who stole), and thus from apparent but undelivered sense into nonsense, imitates the stealth not only of the uncle who moves toward the sleeping king but of the Ghost who in speaking moves his focus from brother to uncle, his blood relative to Hamlet's. (The fact that we in the audience are not likely to notice that grammatical stealth underscores the fact that we do not notice—literally do not see—Hamlet's uncle approach his father sleeping in the orchard: a sleeping father made of words only, an orchard made of words only, an action not performed in the play physically, only in words.)

Other potential but ultimately undelivered sense revolves around the word "stole," whose understood meaning here as an intransitive verb (to move carefully, stealthily) is complicated by its transitive sense (to take dishonestly or secretly), which in this context is appropriate since Claudius did take, "With [that is, by means of] juice of cursed hebona in a vial," his brother's life, crown, and queen. The potential, and potentially active, meanings of "stole" are amplified in the next line by the several possible botanical identifications of "hebona,"[10] the plant whose juice is in the vial, the missing identity of which is a manifestation of the physical absence onstage of said juice in said vial—neither of which can be seen because the event that the Ghost remembers in these words is not performed physically onstage, does not happen in *Hamlet* except in these words.

As the speech continues into the next line and a half, "And in the porches of my ears did pour/The leperous distillment," a complex network of verbal action works to perform the offstage, unperformed physical action that the understood subject from line 61 ("thy uncle") is here said to perform—again, none of this noticed in the theater by anyone watching and listening to the play. Take for example "pour," whose sound repeats the sound of the first syllable in "porches" and is echoed more loosely in the second syllable of "leperous"—this chain of phonetic linkages parallel to the chain of ideas by which liquid ("juice") is transferred from one enclosed space ("vial") to another ("porches"), whereupon it is itself transformed, from "juice" into "distillment." This transformation of the substance poured is echoed in another dimension by a sequence of transformations involving the size and locations of the spaces which contain that substance: the small enclosed space suggested by the "vial" from which "juice" is poured—a space that reduces the size of the enclosure previously suggested by "orchard" (the space within which this action takes place, whose first syllable is echoed in "pour," the verb that conveys the act of moving liquid from one place to another)—which itself implies the presence of a larger enclosure surrounding it (the palm of the hand that holds the vial), continues to pulsate, first expanding as the liquid moves from the "vial" to "porches," whose suggestion of a building greatly enlarges the size of the space suggested by "vial," then by implication being reduced as that liquid moves from the body's entrance ("porches") through its "ears" into its labyrinthine, claustrophobic interior.[11]

Sequential pulsation in space is amplified by a corresponding sequence of temporal actions, since whereas "vial" is singular, both "porches" and "ears" are plural, thus implying a passage of time during which liquid is poured first into one ear, then the other. Visualizing the body asleep in the orchard, the grammar of singular and plural nouns thus invites us to visualize the body asleep, say on its left side (right ear up), which must be turned over by the figure who leans above it in order for him to pour poison into the other ear. The idea of time passing implied by the series of singular followed by plural nouns ("vial," "porches," "ears") is also implicit at the end of this syntactic unit in the noun "distillment," which "juice" becomes once it is poured, whose suggestion of liquid trickling, flowing or falling drop by drop conveys as well the sense of the time during which this slow process must occur.

Although Shakespeare's likely sources (literary and historical) of murder by poison poured into the ears are well known,[12] the significance of the ear as access to the victim's body has, so far as I know, been overlooked. As the port of the body through which sound is perceived, the ear is for acoustic phenomena what the eye is for things visual—threshold, entrance, passageway, door—within or beyond or after which perception can take place. References to ears, physical and figurative, abound in *Hamlet*: "the whole ear of Denmark/Is," according to the Ghost, "Rankly abused" (1.5.36–38) by misinformation given out about how he died; Hamlet calls Rosencrantz and Guildenstern to move closer, becoming "at each ear a hearer" (2.2.325); the sound of Troy crashing in flames "Takes prisoner Pyrrhus' ear" (2.2.417); Hamlet marvels at how the player can "cleave the general ear with horrid speech (2.2.501); in his speech on acting Hamlet warns the players not "to split the ears of the groundlings" (3.2.10); later, in the bedroom scene, showing his mother the pictures of his father and uncle, Hamlet compares the latter to "a mildewed ear / Blasting his wholesome brother" (3.4.63–64), which leads after further verbal assault to Gertrude's "These words like daggers enter in mine ears" (3.4.95). Which brings me back to the Ghost's claim that he was murdered not by daggers piercing his body but by poison poured into his ears: poison embodied in and also analogous to the words he uses to "perform" the physically unperformed offstage action of his death—a death in words only: words the actor who plays the part of the Ghost speaks, which enter (as poison entered the Ghost's body) not just Hamlet's ears but ours too, *Hamlet* itself an imagined port or threshold into death for an audience who hears words "poured" from the mouth of the actor who plays its Ghost.

The embodiment in language of the poison (analogous to those words) that entered King Hamlet's body continues into lines 64–67, where the circuitous syntax and substance of the relative clause works to perform the physical action that its words mean but fail to make materially present. Those words ask us to imagine a "distillment," made in and of words, that enters not just King Hamlet's body but Hamlet's as well: a "distillment"

> whose effect
> Holds such an enmity with blood of man
> That swift as quicksilver it courses through
> The natural gates and alleys of the body.

Like the entrance of this "distillment" into the body (which cannot be seen), a number of verbal "effect[s]" in these lines will not be heard by someone listening to a performance of this speech by an actor: take for instance the two verbs, "Holds" and "courses," both of them present tense but opposite in sense, one meaning to keep or maintain, the other to run through or over (*OED* cites this line as an example of "course" meaning "to run . . . transf. of liquids, etc."). The liquid implied in "courses" continues the idea of liquids running from "juice" to "pour" to "distillment" to "blood" to "quicksilver," and its *or*-sound links it to the verb "pour" by sound as well as sense. Counteracting these ideational and phonetic patterns, the shift in tense from "did pour" to "courses"—a shift already begun in the shift from "stole" (simple past tense) to "did pour" (past auxiliary verb plus present)—makes the action described here as present as the unfolding of words used to describe it.

Moving thus from the "distillment" poured into the ear to its "effect" on the "blood of man"—the phrase, especially in proximity to "body" two lines later, may suggest the Eucharist, another ceremony by which liquid taken into the body is said to produce extraordinary effects, one of which may here be understood as the appearance of this (Holy) Ghost somewhere between the absent Father and grieving Son—the speech again proceeds to shift direction. A syntactic construction in which an initial "effect/Holds such an enmity" invites us to expect a concluding "that" clause, whose subject will be the result of this holding by such an "effect"; instead, although the relative "whose" clause delivers its "that," what follows as a subject in line 66 ("it") appears to be not the result but its cause; not the "effect of "juice" poured into the "ears" but the "juice" itself, which "courses through/The natural gates and alleys of the body."

It is also possible to understand "it" in line 66 as the general "effect" such a liquid has on the body rather than the particular progress of this particular liquid in King Hamlet's body—a general sense that the phrase "blood of man" suggests; and as the passage continues into lines 68–70, the detailed narrative account of what happens as "it"—whatever "it" might refer to—"courses through" the interior of the body continues to support such a reading of "it," meaning both cause ("juice"/"distillment") and "effect":

> And with a sudden vigor it doth posset
> And curd, like eager droppings into milk,
> The thin and wholesome blood.

Variously resonant in the words "posset," "curd," "eager" "droppings," "milk" and "blood,"[13] the idea of liquid that began with "juice" intensifies as the speech begins to focus on exactly what that liquid does to the body it invades—a body whose "blood," formerly "thin and wholesome," suddenly thickens and congeals. The image of curdled milk suggested in "posset/And curd," both of which function here as verbs meaning to coagulate, congeal, or make into a curd or posset, is made explicit in the phrase "like eager droppings into milk," where "eager" functions as an adjective meaning sour or acid, a sense that as Jenkins points out is emphasized by the French spelling in the Folio ("Aigre"). But like the substance it means to make literally present, the grammar of this passage itself seems to curdle, since "eager" also functions here as a noun meaning acid, as the Earl of Rochester first remarked:

The word *egar* is a substantive, and not an adjective: it being a general English name for acids of all kinds. Had the original words been "eager droppings into milk," alluding to the making of sillibubs, the thought would have been inverted; for the milk does not curdle, but is curdled by the acid it is milked upon. Read, therefore, "like *egar, dropping into milk.*"[14]

Rochester is right to notice that it is not the acid that curdles but the milk, a sense made possible only if "eager" is understood as a noun—thus causing "droppings" to function not as plural noun but present participle, which it cannot unless, as Rochester proposes, we drop its final "s."

The physiological "effect" of poison upon the body it invades—poison that causes milk to curdle, "thin and wholesome blood" to clot and clog—is further enacted by a multiplicity of minute, unnoticed (in the theater at least) and substantively insignificant connections that link "eager" and "droppings" to their immediate verbal environment. Consider for instance the following phonetic, grammatical, and ideational coherences and incoherences by which words are pulled simultaneously together and apart. "Eager" shares the sound of "vigor" in the previous line, and if understood as a noun also shares its grammar; if taken as an adjective, it also shares the grammar and some of the meaning of "sudden" in the same position of the previous line, though none of its sound. The plosive-plus-schwa sound in the first syllable of "droppings" links that word to "posset" and "body" as well, but "droppings" and "posset" are opposed ideationally since one suggests upward motion ("to posset" means "to throw up curdled milk"), the other things, or the action of, falling—an idea previously suggested in the speech by "pour" and "distillment," to both of which "droppings" is also ideationally linked. Finally, "eager droppings" and "wholesome blood" are grammatically, metrically and ideationally attracted to one another, since both of these adjective-noun phrases occur in the same positions of their respective lines and both nouns are liquids, but also at the same time ideationally opposed, since their modifying adjectives make the first noun seem "pleasant" (healthy, pure) and the second "unpleasant" (acid, sour, tart). Indeed, the pattern of rhyme-like opposition that connects these two adjectives is part of a larger pattern—unnoticed in the theater—that runs through the passage, positive-sounding adjectives ("my," "secure," "natural," "thin," "wholesome," "smooth") vs. negative-sounding ones ("thy," "cursed," "leperous," "lazarlike," "vile," "loathsome").

A similar pattern of related compound verbs both is and is not continued at the beginning of the next sentence, "So did it mine." But whereas "did . . . mine" appears to repeat the structure of "did pour" and "doth posset," "mine" functions here as a possessive pronoun referring to "blood" rather than a verb meaning to dig a subterranean passage—a verb whose sense nonetheless resonates in this context—thus connecting it by a compound ellipsis to the series of possessive pronoun-plus-noun phrases at the start of the previous sentence: "my orchard," "My custom," "my secure hour," "mine"—both body and blood. This missing but understood presence of "body" and "blood" in "mine" is also amplified by the echo in "So did it" of the entire compound "that" clause in lines 66–70: "that . . . it courses through/The natural gates and alleys of the body/And . . . [that] it doth posset/And curd . . . /The thin and wholesome blood."

The verbal concentration by which a six-line "effect" of "juice"/"distillment" upon the "blood [and body] of man" is reduced to just four words—"So did it mine"—is reversed as the compound sentence begun in line 70 continues:

> And a most instant tetter barked about
> Most lazarlike with vile and loathsome crust
> All my smooth body.

Things get larger rather than smaller here, more intense, "a most instant" for example expanding the scope and increasing the speed implied by "a sudden" in line 68, and "Most lazarlike" adding superlative sense to "leperous" in line 64. The idea of skin implied by "lazarlike"—an idea of the diseased body's exterior surface, which, being seen, stands metonymically for the infected body's interior surfaces, which are not—is amplified by "barked," which, though it functions here as a verb, sounds like the noun meaning tree's skin, "crust," which also suggests skin, and "smooth," which points here to the texture of the healthy body's exterior surface, the skin before it gets infected. Echoing the syntax and some of the sound, but simultaneously counteracting the sense, of "thin and wholesome blood" two lines previously, the phrase "vile and loathsome crust" reaches back through the passage to echo the X "and" Y pattern in both "gates and alleys" and "posset/And curd," whose terms linked by "and" are verbs—which nonetheless also function as nouns—instead of nouns. Finally, "vile" by itself repeats the sound but not the sense of "vial" in line 62—that "vial" whose poison, entering "my smooth body," turns its interior passageways to such "vile . . . crust."[15]

The Ghost's speech pauses for a moment after line 73, "All my smooth body," the silence of whose missing five syllables will direct the actor playing the Ghost to pause for a moment, take a breath, stop talking. After which he will go on for another eighteen lines, to his exit at "Adieu, adieu, adieu. Remember me," after which memory itself takes over as the subject of the play. I too could continue reading his speech, this representation in words of a death that does not physically happen in the play: this "forgèd process of . . . death" we must imagine from the words used to describe it, this "counterfeit presentment" that enables us to "see" something that is not performed onstage—asks us to speculate about what it was that did not happen onstage—and at the same time fails to become, or be, anything *more* than a death in words. But I have gone on long enough, and so I will conclude simply by saying that the presence of accidental, unnoticed (by anyone watching and listening to *Hamlet* performed in the theater, though I have noted them in my "armchair" reading of the play's text), apparently insignificant patterns of interaction among words in this speech dramatize (literally "perform") the offstage world of actions that these words represent: a world that does not exist in the play except in these words, which "hold, as 'twere, the mirror up to nature" (3.2.21–

22), invite us to "see" things with our ears because we cannot see them with our eyes—things we can therefore only speculate about from the words used to "perform" them—words that are in interaction with one another themselves like actors in a text (*Hamlet*) that itself is to the theater as theater is to that text.

4

"There Is a Willow Grows": The Queen's Speech

Audiences do not normally pay much attention to the distinction between what Gertrude Stein called "the thing seen" and "the thing heard"[1]—between physical action performed onstage and acoustic action performed in words. Nor do critics of Shakespeare's plays, whose interpretations inevitably end up talking more about the significance of what happens in the plays—its theoretical, political, historical, cultural, psychological, or dramatic "significance"—than about *how* what happens in words actually happens (*happens*, that is to say, *in words*). Returning again here to the words of *Hamlet* (those "Words, words, words" that Hamlet tells Polonius he is reading; words that are what *Hamlet* itself is ultimately about), I want to look at *how* something that happens offstage (in this case, Ophelia's death) happens in the words of Gertrude's speech:

> There is a willow grows askant the brook,
> That shows his hoary leaves in the glassy stream.
> Therewith fantastic garlands did she make
> Of crowflowers, nettles, daisies, and long purples,
> That liberal shepherds give a grosser name,
> But our cold maids do dead-men's-fingers call them.

There on the pendent boughs her crownet weeds
Clamb'ring to hang, an envious sliver broke,
When down her weedy trophies and herself
Fell in the weeping brook. Her clothes spread wide,
And mermaidlike awhile they bore her up,
Which time she chanted snatches of old lauds,
As one incapable of her own distress,
Or like a creature native and indued
Unto that element. But long it could not be
Till that her garments, heavy with their drink,
Pulled the poor wretch from her melodious lay
To muddy death. (4.7.164–81)

Beyond the questions it raises later in the play—"Is she to be buried in Christian burial when she willfully seeks her own salvation?" (5.1.1-2) the gravedigger asks; "What ceremony else?" (5.1.212, 214) Laertes asks twice; "Her death was doubtful," (216) the priest explains—Gertrude's speech about Ophelia's death has hardly been noted by any of the play's critics.[2] My reading of the speech contends that what happened to Ophelia *is* "doubtful," as the priest says, because Shakespeare doesn't supply anything other than the words of this speech as "evidence" of what "really" happened there on the banks of the stream. That is to say, Shakespeare doesn't show what took place, he has Gertrude tell us; gives us verbal "evidence" at best (either hearsay or an eyewitness account of something that happened elsewhere, offstage); gives only these beautiful words of a speech that *says* (in words) what happened offstage to Ophelia on the banks of the stream—words whose failure to show that action physically onstage leaves us wondering (as other characters in the play also wonder) what exactly it was that took place there. Did Ophelia somehow fall into the stream? Did she take her own life? The questions raised by the gravediggers suggest that questions *are* an appropriate response to Ophelia's death, whose "disappearance" from *Hamlet* in such a speech leaves her strangely "missing in action," visibly memorialized (and beautifully present) in the lush, sensuous, elegiac language of Gertrude's words. And so it is questions, doubt, and uncertainty that I want to think about here: uncertainty about whoever witnessed whatever "really" took place on the banks of that stream; questions about knowing itself, the difficulty of seeing beyond "show"; doubt raised by Gertrude's words, whose lyricism has long been recognized but whose remarkably inconspicuous and (perhaps) revealing details have not until now been noticed.

Let me say before I begin that my reading—an "armchair" reading of verbal effects that will *not* be noticed in the theater by anyone watching and listening to a performance of the play—will take more time and more effort on the part of my reader than it would take the actor who plays Gertrude to deliver this speech. A performance of these eighteen lines of verse in the theater will take about fifty-five seconds by my count, and the reading that follows lasts for some twenty-two pages of prose no actor would want to perform, nor any audience listen to. Nor will the things I am about to talk about be perceived—much less thought about—by anyone in the audience at a performance of *Hamlet* (most of whom have probably also read it on the page, perhaps more than once); indeed, slowing the speech down as much as I mean to do here will not merely derail its train of thought but wreck such a train's dramatic impact: Ophelia, after all, the play's last, best, and indeed only hope for the future of Denmark (who else could bear a child, or heir?), is pronounced dead in this speech. And so, before I begin to "dissect" the beautiful body of Gertrude's speech, let me also say that anyone who has the patience to follow my reading may find reason to think about the questions that I am asking here: What exactly happened offstage? How is it that Gertrude "knows" all of this? Shakespeare doesn't say, gives us no textual "evidence." There is no black box to be recovered from the play, no tape under Claudius's desk. Nor is there a camera in Gertrude's bedroom, nothing to prove she was adulterate (or not) before her first husband's death.[3] Action not performed physically in the play—"performed" in words only—raises questions about what "really" happens in *Hamlet*. The Gertrude who speaks these lines on Ophelia's death (*possibly* knowing more than she discloses here) gives herself away not by protesting too much (she has nothing to protest) but by the play's capacity to take its audience beyond its physical boundary, toward action we cannot see because it "happens" offstage. What is not shown physically cannot ever be known, yet (mysteriously) is wholly imaginable once it enters our ears.

The speech opens by immediately sending our attention somewhere else, away from Gertrude speaking to Laertes and the others who are present onstage, listening to her speak: "There is a willow grows. . . . " "There," which functions here as a pronoun, sounds like and also functions like the adverb "there" (as opposed to "here")—like "there" in Barnardo's question at the beginning of the play ("Who's there?"), which "There is" at the beginning of Gertrude's speech inverts—"there" which is always being somewhere else, "not here." It thus both states the existence of something, or condition, not yet announced and also points toward the site of that existence, a site that is both absent—in our minds offstage to the extent we imagine it—and present in the words used to "show" such "a willow grow[ing] askant the brook."

The word "askant" (which does not occur elsewhere in Shakespeare; the Second Quarto reads "*askaunt*," the Folio "*aslant*") suggests a relationship between the linear trunk of the tree and the linearly flowing brook below it—sidewise, oblique, askew, asquint, according to *OED*'s definition of "askance," which may derive from the Italian *a schiancio* ("bias, slanting, sloping or slopingly, aslope, across, overthwart") and itself suggests a kind of look, view, or point of view. Also like "askew," "askant" suggests an interior state of obliqueness—being off to one side, not quite straight, awry—and with regard to vision, a looking from the side, out of the corners of one's eyes, not straight in the face. In this suggestion of the scene being described as well as of the viewer's perspective, a looking at that scene from the side, it also raises questions: Who has seen this willow beside this brook? Where was that person positioned when the things that Gertrude is about to unfold took place? How has Gertrude come to know about these things in this place?

These questions deserve some comment. It may be that Gertrude was told about Ophelia's death by someone who witnessed it, someone whose words she is now paraphrasing. It may also be that Gertrude witnessed Ophelia's death and so is reporting what she herself saw firsthand, with her own eyes. When Ophelia leaves the play in 4.5, bidding everyone adieu ("Come, my coach! Good night, ladies, good night. Sweet ladies, good night, good night" [71–73]), Claudius gives the order to "Follow her close; give her good watch, I pray you" (74). At this point, the stage direction reads *Exit Horatio* and so we may assume that it is he who departs to carry out the king's command. Is it Horatio who followed Ophelia to the stream where she will drown—Horatio who was the eyewitness of that event? Possibly, though it seems unlikely, since Horatio appears in the very next scene (4.6) speaking to the sailors who give him Hamlet's letter about his return from England, a scene in which Ophelia does not appear. If Horatio is the one who has followed Ophelia out of the king's chamber, he seems by the time of his next appearance in the play not only to have lost sight of her but to have turned his attention toward Hamlet, to whom he makes his way at the end of that scene: "Come, I will give you [the sailors] way for these your letters,/And do't the speedier that you may direct me/To him from whom you brought them" (31–33).

Who then, I want again to ask, has witnessed Ophelia's drowning? And why—given a person who saw that event, saw Ophelia fall or jump into the stream—did he or she not try to rescue her? Why, in other words, is the picture focused exclusively on the object being perceived by the unmentioned witness who must also have been present, the witness some version of whose words Gertrude speaks here? Questions like these have no definitive answers, because Shakespeare does not show what took place on the banks of the stream, gives us instead only Gertrude's words, which are not physical "evidence" of what happened to Ophelia by that stream but, rather, raise the possibility of doubt and uncertainty about what might "really" have happened there.

The second line of Gertrude's speech, "That shows his hoary leaves in the glassy stream," further situates the scene of Ophelia's death. Making the tree masculine, the personal pronoun "his" coupled to "hoary" (the Folio reads "hoar") sounds for a moment like "his whore"—a fleeting misapprehension of the line's sense but one that is pertinent to a play in which the potential sexual promiscuity of the victim who drowns has been of concern to a number of different characters, first to Laertes, who warns her,

> weigh what loss your honor may sustain
> If with too credent ear you list his songs,
> Or lose your heart, or your chaste treasure open
> To his unmastered importunity; (1.3.28–31)

then to her father, who tells her of having learned that Hamlet "hath very oft of late/Given private time to you, and you yourself/Have of your audience been most free and bounteous" (1.3.90–92); and finally then to the man she loves and who, we are led to believe, loves her—a man whose repeated commands to

"Get thee to a nunnery" (3.2.121) order her, punningly at least, to go to a brothel, there to become a whore.[4]

Returning to line 166, if we momentarily misunderstand "hoar-" to be a noun and thus "his hoar-" to be "his whore," then we can further misunderstand "leaves" to be not a noun (leaves on a tree) but a verb (to leave, go out, exit). "Leaves," as a verb, may also sound like "lives," and what follows in the line momentarily, though again misleadingly, supports this: "his whore lives in the glassy stream," which is exactly wrong of course since the stream is where Ophelia loses her life—where she dies. "Leaves," in any case, is not a verb here but a noun: these the willow's leaves, leaves on a tree reflected in the mirror-like surface of the "glassy stream."

Why has this body of water that flows beneath the willow changed from "brook" to "stream," and what is the significance of that shift? For one thing, if we think about how Gertrude is moving the camera around, so to speak, we see that the lines first focus on the tree, then on the water either below or beside it, then on the tree's leaves, then on the image of those leaves reflected in the water. The pattern that links two separate but phonetically-related actions of the tree—it both "*grows* askant the brook" and "*shows* his hoary leaves"—is thus echoed in the ideational pattern that pairs the image of the tree standing in the air with the reflected image of the tree on the surface of the water. In creating two contrasting "views" of the scene, seen as if from two almost simultaneous—but at the same time different—points of view, the first two-line sentence of Gertrude's speech enacts the kind of shift in perspective that the speech itself enacts when it draws our attention away from the stage—away from the character who is speaking these words onstage—toward the site of what it is that she is speaking about. The tree and the image of the tree (an image reflected in "the glassy stream") might also be thought of as being analogous to the scene and the image of the scene (an image reflected in Gertrude's speech): there is, on the one hand, the physical reality of something in the world and on the other a simulacrum of that reality in a visual or verbal representation of it. This "stream" whose surface "shows" the tree thus becomes an image of language itself, which in this case "shows" this scene—the tree, stream, and tree reflected in the stream—to us.

Everything in the first two lines of Gertrude's speech "happens" of course in far less time than I have just taken to describe it— indeed happens in the time it takes the actor playing Gertrude to say these two lines, no more than ten seconds I would guess. At the same time, the fact that we do not notice (don't even notice that we don't notice) the complexity of the physics by which words create a picture of what is not being performed onstage, a picture that "shows" action imagined in an unseen world that its word-enactment here "represents," is crucial to our experience of a play obsessed with how things we do not see onstage, because they aren't performed physically, take place literally (i.e., verbally) in the language that *Hamlet* uses to "show" them.

Gertrude's speech continues in a four-line sentence that focuses on the person beside the stream and what it is that she does there:

> Therewith fantastic garlands did she make
> Of crowflowers, nettles, daisies, and long purples,
> That liberal shepherds give a grosser name,
> But our cold maids do dead-men's-fingers call them.
> (166–69)

"Therewith," in echoing "There is" at the start of the speech, sounds for a moment as if Gertrude is returning to where she began. Instead, her subject being the "she" that is (or was) Ophelia, she launches into an account of an action that, although it takes her only a few moments to describe, must have taken Ophelia awhile to carry out (she did not make just one garland but "garlands"—

at least two, maybe more, something that must have required her not only to gather the several kinds of flowers she used but to sit beside the stream and weave them together). (The Folio reads "Therewith fantastic garlands did she come," suggesting that Ophelia has arrived at the stream with her garlands already made, having picked and woven them.) The word "fantastic" recalls Ophelia's grief-stricken madness in 4.5, the last time she appears alive in the play,[5] as does the list of flowers she weaves into "garlands"—"Crowflowers, nettles, daisies, and long purples"—which clearly echo the rosemary, pansies, fennel, daisy, columbine, rue, and violets that she handed out to those who witnessed that scene. At the same time, the fact that Gertrude now speaks a "language of flowers" also connects *her* to Ophelia, who was in her madness fluent in that language. Thus strangely paired by their language, Gertrude and Ophelia participate in a relationship that places them in close proximity to one another: one the speaker and the other the person she herself was looking at, the object of her gaze.[6]

The flowers Ophelia weaves into "garlands" (or arrives with, according to the Folio text) suggest a range of significant and at times contradictory associations. "Crowflowers," a popular English name for various species of buttercup (family *Ranunculaceae*), are related to the crowfoot, or wild hyacinth (family *Nymphaeceae*), whose name suggests not only the crow's feet surrounding squinting eyes—and by extension the person who watches this scene—but the girl-nymph being watched and the wet, marshy streambank where this flower grows and this scene takes place. The long *o* sound of the first syllable of "crowflowers" links that word to "shows" in the same position of line 165, an echo that works to emphasize the implicit physical relationship between what is being seen (these flowers, this willow "That shows his hoary leaves") and the person to whom, in this act of seeing, this scene is being "shown." "[N]ettles" stands alone in this company of otherwise pleasant-sounding flowers—in each of the other eleven passages in which nettles (family *Urticaceae*) appear, Shakespeare foregrounds that plant's ability to sting,[7] a property that literally embodies the emotional bite of a speech whose tragic end Gertrude has previewed when she reports, "Your sister's drowned, Laertes" (4.7.162). It is thus also connected to "willow" (proverbially weeping) at the start of the speech, these two plants joined in opposition to "crowflowers" and "daisies"[8] (*bellis perennis*), which—literally surrounding "nettles" in the line ("crowflowers, nettles, daisies")—are paired as much for their pleasing associations as "nettles" and "willows" are for their abilities either to produce physical pain or to register its emotional sting.

The few early instances of conjecture about exactly which flowers Shakespeare meant by "long purples"[9] fail to notice how much attention Gertrude pays to this flower in relation to the other three. While "crowflowers," "nettles," and "daisies" are each mentioned in passing, so to speak, the "long purples" that Ophelia weaves into her garlands lead to a two-line relative clause that raises and attempts to decide between two of the names people commonly give to that flower. Although a "purple" is a kind of flower, the word "purple" in its thirteen other appearances in Shakespeare has more often than not to do with blood than with flowers.[10] Gertrude's list of flowers is thus also composed of an alternating ABAB series that pairs "crowflowers" and "daisies"— linked not only by their beauty but implicit references to sight (crowsfeet, "day's eye")—opposed to "nettles" and "long purples," one causing pain and the other "showing" its color (i.e., blood coming out of the body).

The negative spin inherent in the word "purples," which is not only a flower but "a disease characterized by an eruption of purplish pustules,"[11] is amplified as Gertrude goes on to talk about these flowers, "That liberal shepherds give a grosser name, / But our cold maids do dead-men's-fingers call them." It turns out that "long purples" is one of three names given to this flower, two of which appear in the play and the other of which ("a grosser name") is conspicuous by its absence. So are the shepherds who use this name, and so are those "cold maids" (the Second Quarto reads "cull-cold maids") who, though missing from the play, nonetheless lead an audience to think inevitably of the drowned Ophelia, who is herself now missing. The means by which Gertrude links Ophelia, who is dead, to the name of the flower she wove into garlands by the stream she drowned in—a flower that Ophelia-like "cold maids" ("cold" suggesting both chasteness and death) call "dead-men's-fingers" and that "liberal [male] shepherds give a grosser name"—will, once again, *not* be noticed by anyone watching the play in the theater. As such, these verbal effects are *like* the offstage, physically unperformed (and thus unseen) actions that they describe: what we *hear* (but don't recognize we are hearing) and what we *hear about* (but don't ever actually see performed onstage) being in effect Shakespeare's way in *Hamlet* of calling into question how it is that we know what we know; how it is in this case that words can "show" things they do *not* show—even as they also inevitably fail to "show" those things, things we don't actually see.

The synonym for "long purples" that is "a grosser name" having been cut from Gertrude's speech, we in the audience must speculate about just what these "liberal shepherds" would call such a flower.[12] But were the people who use such names present at the scene of the drowning, and if so did they use such names in the account of Ophelia's actions that they gave to Gertrude—did she hear them use such names in other words, and then purposefully delete them from her own present account of that event? Or is Gertrude herself ad-libbing here—is she familiar with the colloquial, and in this case off-color, language of the so-called "liberal shepherds" who, we assume from this speech, inhabit the country-side around Elsinore? If the two-line relative clause that follows "long purples" is simply Gertrude's digression, as on the surface it would appear to be, its vaguely sinister (and not so vaguely sexual) overtones also appear to further the increasingly disquieting sense that runs below the surface of her report about what happened to Ophelia. Everything that happened took place "elsewhere," but the way the setting of that event is being dramatized here, "re-staged" in Gertrude's words, shadows what actually happened, ma-nipulates it as much as the "fingers" on the hands of "dead men" can.

One way of understanding the scene that Gertrude's language unfolds here is to see that "our cold maids" (and by implicit sug-gestion Ophelia), who avoid the "grosser name" that "liberal shep-herds give" to the flowers Gertrude calls "long purples" by calling them "dead-men's-fingers," are themselves made "cold" by those men—either because as chaste women (like Ophelia) they resist the sexual advances of their aggressive male counterparts, or because those men's fingers have strangled or at least killed them. Nothing in her speech explicitly states such a relationship between Ophelia or those maids, those men, or this speaker. Nor does Gertrude mean to imply that any sort of relationship between Ophelia and anyone—anyone who may have been watching her, be it "liberal shepherds," followers from the court or Gertrude herself—actu-ally took place on the banks of the stream beside which that "wil-low grows." (As one instance of the multiple uncertainties in the speech, notice that a phonetic likeness of "grows" and the first syl-lable of "grosser" is countered by an ideational near-opposition between "grows," which suggests life, and the "grosser name" maids avoid by calling such flowers "dead-men's-fingers," which suggest not only death but—crossing gender lines—Ophelia's death; notice also that the play between "grows" and the first syllable of "grosser" enriches, with the ideas of vegetable vitality and animalistic, shameful sex, the name which cold maids like dead Ophelia use, "dead-men's-fingers.") At the same time, nothing in the speech is entirely innocent, straightforward, or even clear, untainted by the possibility that something more than what Gertrude says—more than meets the ear here—has happened: Who saw this offstage action? Who told Gertrude about it? How does she know these things?

Another way of reading the picture sketched out by Gertrude's language is to listen further to the sound it makes. Although nothing about the sound patterns I am about to describe in the first six lines of this speech can be called unusual (nor will they call any attention to themselves in a performance of *Hamlet* in the theater, where no one is likely to notice that they even exist), at least not in a passage noted for being as "poetical" as this one,[13] the density of sound relationships in the speech is nonetheless remarkable, in that it "imagines" aurally the physical relationships among the people who are explicitly and implicitly present in the scene being described—people whose relationships pull them simultaneously together and apart as much as the sounds of the words Gertrude uses to describe them do. Words that in various ways sound alike do not of course constitute "evidence" that something other than what such words "say" has taken place. Nor can the sounds of words that in proximity to one another create ordinary sound patterns in English—even the sounds of words in Shakespeare's highly patterned English—be taken to signify anything about what those words mean (to say that "Fred lies on the bed with the red spread" does not mean he was murdered there). Still, whatever "happened" on the banks of the stream seems less certain than the "evidence" of Gertrude's speech suggests, especially given the relationships between certain of the words she uses to report those events, words whose phonetic relations "echo" (literally "amplify") connections in other systems of order relevant to the question of how Ophelia died.

Like the echo of "grows" in "grosser," the contrast of whose implied meanings works to pull those words apart as much as their rhyme-like phonetic identity pulls them together, the sound of the word "name" in the phrase "a grosser name" echoes in reverse the *m*-plus-long *a* sounds in "make" at the end of line 166, creating a rhyme-like attraction between that pair of lines, the first of which talks about what Ophelia did beside the stream (she made garlands) and the second of which names (even as it refuses to name) one of the kinds of flowers she used to make those garlands. The vowel-plus-*m* pattern in "name" also echoes a similar pattern in "them" at the end of the following line, a pronoun that refers to the "long purples" whose "liberal shepherds['s] . . . grosser name" Gertrude, for whatever reason, keeps to herself, although she freely enough reports their alternate name—"dead-men's-fingers"—a name that itself seems "grosser" than "long purples." The short *e* sounds in "dead-men's-fingers" links that name of the flower to the same sound in "them," the pronoun that again refers to the earlier name of that flower, "long purples," whose *ur* sound followed by a ter-minal *s* is echoed in "fingers" and "shepherds." Those "shepherds" are also related by gender to the "dead men" whose "fingers" they share sound effects with, a connection made aurally emphatic by their shared short *e* sounds—hardly a noticeable echo, not at least in the theater, but nonetheless present no matter how likely we are *not* to notice it. At the same time, "shepherds" is related by its terminal *ds* sound to "maids," a phonetic link that contradicts their opposition by gender and by the alternative names they each give to the flower (one of which Gertrude refuses to give). The sup-pressed "grosser name" that "liberal shepherds" call the flowers

Gertrude calls "long purples" thus sounds, in the alternate name—
"dead-men's-fingers"—given to it by "our cold maids," not only
like Gertrude's name for that flower but also like the men who
call it something else (whose body parts that name refers to), men
whose name ("shepherds") variously sounds like the other name
those "maids" call it ("dead-men's-fingers").

Let me say again that what I am describing—relationships between little noises in a few lines of a play—will happen in far less
time in the theater than I have taken to describe them here. What
is more, the things I am describing here will not be noticed by
anyone watching *Hamlet* in the theater. Sound effects, including
those that connect words variously linked together in other systems of order, simply happen too quickly and too constantly for us
to notice that they *are* happening. And yet they are there, clearly
and effectively present—on the page, in the air/ear—sounding,
and available to be heard and noticed (even if not consciously),
whenever *Hamlet* is performed. Indeed, the fact that we do not
consciously notice them in the theater is why they are so aesthetically effective: sound events that we do not notice are themselves
like offstage events that we do not see, which those sound events as
such "perform," literally "show" us.

Picking up the action where she had left off, Gertrude's speech
continues to report what Ophelia did—or what was done to her—
in the setting thus far described:

> There on the pendent boughs her crownet weeds
> Clamb'ring to hang, an envious sliver broke,
> When down her reedy trophies and herself
> Fell in the weeping brook.

As her sentence unfolds, the absence of Gertrude's supposed third
person subject ("she" or "Ophelia," whose "crownet weeds [she
was now] Clamb'ring to hang") enacts grammatically the absence of that subject's action on the banks of the stream—that is,

Ophelia's failure not only to hang her "crownet weeds" on those "pendent boughs" but to hang there herself. Which is not to suggest that Ophelia hanged herself or was even hanged by someone else but rather to point to the multiple contradictory suggestions of a statement that appears to state what everyone who hears that statement understands to be clear and obvious even though it is not: climbing the willow tree from which she wanted to hang the flowers she had woven into garlands, Ophelia fell or jumped into the water. Hearing this speech, that is what we understand happened to her, even though the speech does not make what we understand has happened to her appear to be what must have happened. (If, as Gertrude states, "an envious sliver broke," it would seem clear that Ophelia slipped rather than jumped, yet the gravedigger's question in the following scene about whether Ophelia will be given a Christian burial if "she drowned herself" will soon undermine that conclusion.)

The grammatical subject of the sentence, a subject apparently modified by the preceding participial phrase ("on the pendent boughs . . . / Clamb'ring to hang"), turns out to be "an envious sliver," which does not make sense. (Strictly speaking, Gertrude's sentence will only make grammatical sense if we understand her subject to be the missing but implied "she" or "Ophelia" whose verb is "broke" and whose object is "sliver"—"trying to hang her flowers on the branch of the tree, [she/Ophelia] broke a branch"— a reading that transforms what seems to be the subject and motive of this action ["an envious sliver"] into an object whose motive in that construction [envy] again makes no sense.) And even if we try to make grammatical sense of Gertrude's sentence by understanding a missing but implied "she" or "Ophelia" acting as the subject—"[she/Ophelia], attempting to hang her flowers on the branch of the tree, broke that branch"—we are still faced with a narrative time scheme that makes the result of the branch breaking (Ophelia's fall into the stream) happen *before* the branch itself breaks: that is, while the falling of those flowers and that person takes place in the narrative sequence *after* "an envious sliver broke," the force of the adverbial "when" clause ("When down her weedy trophies and herself / Fell . . . ") makes the action of falling appear to cause, and therefore precede, the breaking of the branch.

My point in getting lost in the grammatical and chronological confusions of Gertrude's sentence is to propose again that what happened beside the stream and what happens in the language that describes those actions in that setting take place in two different "locations"—one the world and the other words—that, in so far as one precedes the other in time and took place in a decidedly different space than the one Gertrude uses to describe it, may or indeed may not coincide. What took place and what we hear as Gertrude speaks about it are not necessarily equal to one another—are necessarily *not equal* in fact, since one took place in the world and the other in Gertrude's representation of it, a world of words whose "evidence" seems to call everything that happened there into question.

The terms of that world take on an even more uncertain perspective if we begin to look at their spatial interrelationship, not only in Gertrude's language but also in the scene that language describes. The word "crownet," for instance, suggests the wreath of flowers that Ophelia has woven from her collection of "crowflowers" (which "crownet" may echo phonetically), "nettles" (which "crownet" echoes in another way), "daisies" (which "crownet" echoes ideationally, the circular shape of the wreath a larger and/ or smaller variation on the round shape of the daisy [and/or day's eye]), and "long purples" (which "crownet" again echoes ideationally, the royalty it implies—the Folio reads "coronet"—in effect repeating the sense of royalty traditionally associated with the color purple. It also suggests not only Christ's crown of thorns (*OED* 2b)—a meaning also suggested by "garland" (*OED* 1b) and one that has often been thought of as particularly appropriate to Ophelia—and the "crowner" (coroner) who will be mentioned in the next scene, but the royal crown that Gertrude, as Queen of Denmark, may herself be wearing as she gives this speech. To follow the implications of that suggestion a bit further, it might be possible to trace a line of verbal events in which Ophelia, "Clamb'ring to hang" Gertrude's "crownet" in the tree—attempting that is to make her way up in the world by marrying the queen's son and thereby assuming claim to her crown—dies because, jealous of such an attempt by a low-born girl both to improve her social position ("Lord Hamlet is a prince, out of thy star" (2.2.141), as even her father says) and, even more threatening, to cause a son to transfer his love for his mother to the woman who will become his wife, "an envious sliver" of that tree "broke."

The possibility that Gertrude herself may be "envious" of Ophelia is suggested by other elements in these lines, which also call little attention to themselves. The phonetic and etymological history by which Ophelia's "crownet"/coronet is connected to the crown Gertrude wears is matched by a pair of associations that connect both "pendent" (from the Latin *pendere*, to hang) to "hang" and "boughs" (from Old English *bog*, related to Old Norse *bogr*, shoulder) to "fingers"—connect, that is, the woven crown of flowers that Ophelia tries to hang in the tree to the hanging branches of the tree itself, one of which when it breaks sends her into the "brook"—which is itself related phonetically and etymologically to the verb "broke."[14] This linkage between "brook . . . broke . . . brook" is one of several such chains in the speech, each of which suggests meanings beyond the power of any single element in the chain to suggest, implications beyond the scope of what Gertrude herself means to convey when she tells Laertes where and how his "sister . . . drowned." And yet these chains of fleeting connections between the words of the speech are there, not noticed in the theater and all the more effective for that reason, in that they "perform" (in language) the missing (i.e., unseen, thus likewise "unnoticed") offstage action they refer to. Take for instance the chain of tree-related words ("willow . . . leaves . . . boughs . . . sliver"), words related by extension to "weeping," commonly associated with willow trees, though "weeping" is here transferred to describe, in its pathetic fallacy, the stream beside which that weeping willow grows—the stream whose flowing water is itself like tears.There is also the even longer chain of flower-related words ("garlands . . . crowflowers, nettles, daisies . . . long purples . . . dead-men's-fingers . . . crownet weeds . . . weedy trophies"), words pointing to "real things" in the world that trace Ophelia's "progress" through Gertrude's story—from making "garlands" beside the tree, to her attempt to hang "crownet weeds" in the tree, to falling (or jumping) with her "weedy trophies" into the stream.

When Ophelia falls into the stream she does not fall by herself; she is preceded, at least in the chronology of events in Gertrude's speech, by the flowers she has woven into wreathes: "her weedy trophies and herself / Fell." The logic by which "crownet weeds" becomes "weedy trophies" is puzzling, particularly in light of the fact that each pair in the chiasmus—the round "crownet," a noun used here as an adjective modifying "weeds," which become an adjective modifying "trophies," a word derived in its turn from "trope," meaning "to turn"—is itself the object of the possessive pronoun "her" ("her crownet weeds . . . her weedy trophies"), a series that itself is completed by the last but not least element that falls into the stream, "herself." Finally, although undercut by vaguely negative associations in "weeds" and "weedy," the suggestion of power, privilege, position, and victory in "crownet" and "trophies"—which sound like overtones in words whose appearance in phrases parallel to "her" links them to Ophelia herself ("her *crownet* weeds . . . her weedy *trophies* . . . her*self*")—appears to connect Ophelia, the subject of this speech, to Gertrude herself, who is now reporting this news of Ophelia's offstage death.

What happened next to Ophelia must have taken much longer than the next sentence of Gertrude's speech takes to describe it:

> Her clothes spread wide,
> And mermaidlike awhile they bore her up,
> Which time she chanted snatches of old lauds,
> As one incapable of her own distress,
> Or like a creature native and indued
> Unto that element.

Though it seems straightforward enough, this summary of what took place following Ophelia's fall into the water is remarkable not only for its suggestion of slow-motion, static calm—the calm pictured in John Everett Millais's great painting "Ophelia"—but for the sexual overtones of "clothes spread wide"[15] and for its failure to describe the physical action it appears to describe. We do not actually *see* Ophelia in the water—where she floats "awhile," apparently long enough to sing "snatches" of songs[16]—do not see the person whose body has fallen into "that element." Rather, we see her "clothes"—generic, sexually suggestive, and disembodied—"spread wide . . . mermaidlike"—a transformation difficult to picture: what clothes was she wearing when she fell into the stream, and have they changed, or changed her, into a fish? Though she implies several times that time is passing, Gertrude does not tell us how long Ophelia floats there in the water—how long was "awhile" and "Which time," how long those "snatches" of the songs she sings? They might have been very short; however, they might have gone on for quite some time, long enough for whoever witnessed this scene to hear what Ophelia "chanted" and identify it as pieces of "old lauds" or hymns.[17] While the songs that Ophelia sang in her mad scene were not "lauds," the fact that we heard her sing them makes it seem possible that she was still singing *something* in that moment of "her own distress"—the moment immediately preceding her death. Having walked out of that previous scene singing a death song—"And will a not come again? . . . God 'a' mercy on his soul" (4.5.184, 193)—she seems to have continued singing as if uninterrupted, as if her singing of those songs had not stopped until the moment of her last breath. But exactly what she sang while floating in water "like a creature native and indued / Unto that element" we do not know.

Nor will we find out, because Gertrude's account of the songs Ophelia sang "snatches" of fails to name or quote from them. Indeed, the songs that Ophelia sings are cut off—Ophelia's breath stopped—by what happens next in Gertrude's speech:

> But long it could not be
> Till that her garments, heavy with their drink,
> Pulled the poor wretch from her melodious lay
> To muddy death.

In Gertrude's account of it, the clothes that "mermaidlike" enabled Ophelia's body to float on the surface of the water now, having absorbed that same water, cause her to sink. The person who had just been described as a "creature" apparently at home in the water becomes a "poor wretch" who, instead of floating in what had been a "glassy stream," is now "Pulled . . . To muddy death."

Such apparently inconsequential shifts as these—shifts like the one by which "creature native" becomes "poor wretch" and water so "glassy" that its surface reflects the willow's leaves becomes "muddy" as it pulls the body of the victim down—may be taken as "evidence" of the play's persistent refusal to "show" us action that "happened" offstage and, therefore, the difficulty of knowing what did indeed "happen" there: who did what to whom, how (and why) Ophelia died. Watching *Hamlet* in the theater, we don't see what isn't performed physically onstage; likewise, we also don't "hear" (don't notice *consciously*, that is, though we do in fact hear them) "duplicities" of sound and word meaning such as the following ones—ordinary enough to be sure and all the more remarkable for that reason. "[L]ong" in the phrase "long purples" (the common name of a flower, suggestive of size in space), for example, is not the same "long" at the start of the last sentence of Gertrude's speech, "But long it could not be," where it refers to some time rather than space or flowers—the time Ophelia floated and sang. Similarly, "that" in the phrase "Unto that element" is not the same "that" as the one in the same position in the following line, "Till that her garments," where it functions grammatically not as an adjective but a conjunction that is both semantically unnecessary (we understand "until her garments") and grammatically deceptive ("that her garments," which here may be understood as an ellipsis for "until that time," does not make sense, whereas "those her garments" would). (Each of these "that"'s is also different from the ones that have previously appeared as relative conjunctions in the phrases "That shows his hoary leaves" and "That liberal shepherds," both of which are both connected and disconnected to the relative conjunction in the phrase "Which time she chanted.") Similarly, the word "garments" (which echoes some of the sounds but not sense of "garlands") itself participates in a series of semantic relationships with "weeds" (one of whose meanings is clothes), "indued" (one of whose meanings is to be clothed) and, most directly, with the "clothes [that] spread wide, / And . . . bore her up," whereas these "garments, being heavy with their drink, / Pulled" the body down. The word "bore," meaning here to float, suggests in another of its meanings (to give birth to, to bear a child) an entrance to life directly opposed to the exit from life ("To muddy death") that is about to take place in "that element" Ophelia seemed for a moment to be "native" (again born) to. The place of that death is called by many names—"brook," "stream," "brook" (again), "that element," and finally "drink," a word that suggests both the water that swallows Ophelia's body and the water that Ophelia's clothes swallow, after which she sinks. Whereas she "Fell" from a tree when "an envious sliver broke" (by accident it would seem), she is in the end "Pulled . . . /To muddy death," as if unseen hands under the water are dragging her down. The moment she goes under, the "melodious lay" she was singing stops— though it is singular, we understand "lay" to mean songs; we also understand it to mean what it does not mean in the phrase "melodious lay" (the prone position of the body floating on the water's surface, which then sinks into it); so too do those "snatches" she had previously "chanted," each of which must also have been interrupted (stopped). Indeed, the phrase "chanted snatches" is a kind of mini-enactment of the physics of that interruption, the phonetic scrambling of one word in the other ("chanted" is a near-anagram of "snatches") demonstrating in a microcosm how "snatches" (Ophelia's songs, Shakespeare's text) might be broken apart, put together, articulated, "chanted."

Finally, I would ask again how it is that Gertrude knows what she knows—the detailed description of the landscape, the action Ophelia took there, the songs she sang, the way she slipped beneath the water. And in stepping back from the unseen scene of Ophelia's death to ask who witnessed what amounts to a series of separate actions—who saw and/or heard her weave, climb, hang, fall, float, sing, and finally sink—I want again to shift the focus of attention from the person being perceived to the person (or persons) who perceived her. For unless Gertrude is making all of this up, the specificity of detail (i.e., concrete, physical "things") in her speech implies the presence of an eyewitness observer, someone standing on the riverbank who watched—but did not intervene in—the series of actions leading to the death of the girl. Who was that person and why did he or she do nothing to save her?

Gertrude does not say, nor does she suggest that she was that witness. But if we question the identity of the implicitly present (however unmentioned) eyewitness who saw the event, it seems possible that something more than meets the eye or in this case ear—more than an innocent girl's accidental drowning—took place at the scene of that event. Rendered in the beauty of Gertrude's language, the spectacle drew whoever saw it to notice everything: willow reflected in the surface of the mirror-like stream, "fantastic garlands" of assorted native flowers, Ophelia and her "weedy trophies" falling through space, her "clothes spread wide" bearing her up, her disembodied voice singing "snatches" of songs. What Gertrude's words do not record is the eyewitness who saw it happen—either Gertrude who delivers the speech or else an unnamed person who told her what happened. Which raises further questions: Why, if it was Gertrude, was she there? Why, if it was someone else, doesn't she let us know? Shakespeare is mute on this point, doesn't say how the messenger knows what she knows—which is reasonable enough, since he needs to move his story forward at this point, and Gertrude-as-messenger is as good a way to remove Ophelia from the play as anything. But it may still leave us wondering about the mysterious figure standing there in the bushes, who did nothing to rescue poor Ophelia—"killed" here in Gertrude's speech, whose rhetorical production of the illusion of "evidence" invites us to "see" something that isn't "shown," an offstage death whose details appear only in these words, whose "evidence" is all that Shakespeare gives us of that mysterious, reported event.

Had Shakespeare chosen to show that scene, there would not be any question about what happened to Ophelia on the banks of that stream. We would have seen clear, unambiguous, visible, physical actions: either the branch breaks or she accidentally slips or she jumps, case closed. Because he chose *not* to show it but to represent it in words only, he leaves the door open for us to speculate about what "really" happened offstage. Did the branch break? Did she fall or jump? Or was she perhaps pushed? Not showing what happened, the play's words leave us with a sense of doubt, ambiguity, and uncertainty about the actions those words mean to represent. And that is the point, since uncertainty ("Who's there?"), ambiguity ("To be or not to be" [3.1.56]), and the unknowableness of death ("The undiscovered country from whose bourn/No traveler returns" [3.1.79–80]) are among the play's central concerns—concerns mirrored, and literally sounded, in the ambiguity and uncertainty of passages like this one.

5

"T'Have Seen What I Have Seen": The Two Closet Scenes

Among the actions that do not take place on the stage of *Hamlet* except in words—King Hamlet's death in the orchard, which the Ghost describes in 1.5; Ophelia's death in the stream, which Gertrude describes in 4.7; Hamlet's voyage to England, which Hamlet tells Horatio about in 5.2—is the action of sex: specifically, sex between Gertrude and Claudius, which Hamlet "performs" (in words only) when he pleads with his mother not to "Let the bloat king tempt you again to bed" (3.4.182), and sex between Hamlet and Ophelia, which Ophelia "performs" (in words only) when she tells Polonius what happened when Hamlet "[came] before [her]" "while [she] was sewing in [her] closet" (2.1.83, 76). In this chapter I talk about the performance of action in these two speeches—the verbal action *in* the speech, the physical action described *by* it—action whose absent presence and present absence suggests the degree to which action in the theater is always both visual and acoustic, a matter of seeing and hearing. My assumptions are (1) that Ophelia's and Hamlet's speeches are "performative" in Austin's sense ("the issuing of the utterance is the performing of an action"[1]), not *contractual* (Austin's example of this is "I bet") or *declar-*

atory ("I declare war") but literally *demonstrative*—enactments in words—of the offstage action they appear to describe, and *do* describe, but also at the same time "perform," in and by means of the action (interaction) of words; (2) that the verbal performance of offstage, physical action in the two closet scenes—"remembered" when Ophelia speaks to her father, "imagined" and/or "projected" when Hamlet speaks to his mother—"shows" us, and invites us to "see," something we do not actually see except to the extent that we imagine it in the words used to "perform" it; and (3) that the physically unseen action of sex pictured in Ophelia's words to her father and Hamlet's words to his mother brings us face to face with what *Hamlet* is about: not sex but words themselves, how words work to enact a world whose meaning cannot be seen or heard, a world whose performance in the theater becomes, as Hamlet (in the Folio) says of "nothing," what "thinking makes . . . so" (2.2.250).

To begin with a portrait painted by Jan van Eyck one hundred fifty years before the time of *Hamlet: Giovanni Arnolfini and His Bride* shows, according to H. W. Janson, "[t]he young couple . . . solemnly exchanging marriage vows in the privacy of the bridal chamber."[2] There appears to be no one else present in the room, but, as Janson points out, reflected in a small round mirror "conspicuously placed behind them" on the wall is the image of two other figures, one of whom must be the artist, since the words "Johannes de eyck fuit hic" (Jan van Eyck was here) is written "in florid legal lettering" above the date, 1434. The painter is a witness to this marriage ceremony, his painting a kind of "pictorial marriage certificate." Although Janson goes on to talk about the symbolism of several of the picture's details—the single candle in the chandelier that, burning in broad daylight, "stands for the all-seeing Christ"; the couple's shoes, which they have taken off to "remind us that they are standing on 'holy ground'"; a small dog, which is "an emblem of marital faith"—what he does not tell us is that Giovanni Arnolfini's bride is pregnant, her left hand resting on her noticeably rounded belly across which falls the folds of her long green dress, the perfectly-made-up scarlet cover of the canopied marriage bed behind her only apparently still waiting for the supposed consummation of the wedding night to take place.

In pointing to the figure of the bride in the van Eyck portrait, which may have been intended to prove that Giovanni Arnolfini's bride was indeed capable of producing the heirs that he would naturally have wanted, together with the figure of the painter reflected in the mirror behind the couple, I want to suggest several parallels to *Hamlet*: (1) that the absent presence of the painter reflected in the mirror is analogous to the absent presence of Shakespeare the author who wrote the play (and perhaps played the part of its ghost) and to his audience in the theater, who watches the unfolding of its action; (2) that the bridal chamber itself, in which only the wedding couple seems to be present (no other witnesses), is like the site of offstage action in *Hamlet* (likewise no eyewitnesses); and (3) that Giovanni Arnolfini's noticeably pregnant bride imagines a *possible* picture of Ophelia herself—who may also be pregnant, can be *imagined* as being pregnant, even though there is no concrete "evidence" in the play to prove it. And that is exactly the point: there is no evidence for actions that happen offstage in the play except for the play's words, which are "circumstantial evidence," subject always to interpretation, uncertainty, and doubt. What Shakespeare has left out of *Hamlet* cannot ever quite be known definitively, which is part of why *Hamlet* continues to be so fascinating. And so while I can't prove Ophelia is pregnant—Shakespeare certainly gives no concrete evidence that she is—neither, I think, can that unlikely possibility be disproved. Directors, actors, audiences, readers—we continue to make interpretations of the play

that are necessarily speculative, inevitably subject to further interpretation by someone else.

If we imagine that Ophelia is indeed pregnant at the time of her
death, then we may also ask when Hamlet and Ophelia could have
had sex. Certainly not onstage during the time of the play, though
their exchange in *The Mousetrap* scene is filled with sexually loaded
language that may be taken as "evidence" of a certain relaxed familiarity between them:

> HAMLET Lady, shall I lie in your lap?
> OPHELIA No, my Lord.
> [HAMLET I mean, my head upon your lap?
> OPHELIA Ay, my lord.]
> HAMLET Do you think I meant country matters?
> OPHELIA I think nothing, my lord.
> HAMLET That's a fair thought to lie between maids'
>   legs.
> OPHELIA What is, my lord?
> HAMLET Nothing. (3.2.110–16 [lines in bracket ap-
>   pear in Folio])

—"circumstantial evidence" at best, which "proves" nothing but
nonetheless may be taken for what it is: Shakespeare asking his
audience to notice the sexual implications of this language, to
read between the lines so to speak, to think about what it means
or where these words are coming from or why Hamlet speaks
this way to Ophelia.[3] But sometime offstage during the time of
the play, or prior to the play, it would have been *possible*—I am
speculating here of course, because the play "shows" nothing of
this—for Hamlet and Ophelia to have had sex. Certainly we hear
Ophelia was spending time with Hamlet ("'Tis told me he hath
very oft of late / Given private time to you, and you yourself / Have
of your audience been most free and bounteous" [1.3.90–92], as
Polonius says to Ophelia; then a few lines later Ophelia uses the
same words to confess that Hamlet has indeed been courting her:

"He hath, my lord, of late made many tenders/Of his affection to me" [98–99]). But when did these things happen, what might it mean for Ophelia to have "been most free and bounteous" of her "audience," and for Hamlet to have "made many tenders of his affections to [her]"—what exactly has been going on?[4]

In raising the question about offstage relations between Hamlet and Ophelia, I am again asking about things we cannot know, not just because we do not *see* them performed but because Shakespeare did not include them in the play. But unlike the play's originary offstage action—the death of King Hamlet, which happens before the play begins and from which everything that happens in the play follows—there is no re-play of the missing action between Hamlet and Ophelia, no reenactment as with King Hamlet's death first in the Ghost's speech, then in the dumb show, and then in *The Mousetrap*, nothing to show us what might have taken place when "Lord Hamlet" came to Ophelia "as [she] was sewing in [her] closet,"

> with his doublet all unbraced,
> No hat upon his head, his stockings fouled,
> Ungartered, and down-gyvèd to his ankle,
> Pale as his shirt, his knees knocking each other,
> And with a look so piteous in purport
> As if he had been loosèd out of hell
> To speak of horrors—   (2.1.76–83)

Nor, if there were any other offstage encounters, as it seems there were judging from what she has told Polonius about the "many tenders/Of his affections" that Hamlet has "of late made . . . to me," is there any direct, visible, performed "evidence" of those encounters—nothing, that is, except those "remembrances" that Ophelia has "longèd long to redeliver" to Hamlet (3.1.93–94), "remembrances" that may be understood to stand for things that have happened between them before the play began (or during the time of the play), the times they have spent together, their glances and words and physical contact (if any).

If everything in Hamlet and Ophelia's offstage experience is embodied in the "remembrances" she holds in her hand in 3.1, those props—letters, flowers, pictures, whatever they might be— become especially important in any performance of the play. As physical evidence of events in their relationship that are not performed onstage, these flowers (they must be dried now) or pictures (plural, because "remembrances" is plural, of Hamlet?) or letters or bracelets or rings or necklaces (a locket with his picture in it?) or books (she must be holding at least the one that Polonius has given her just before setting her loose to meet Hamlet) take on the power of a crystal ball, through which we in the audience are invited to think about what isn't performed, what might have happened between Hamlet and Ophelia. What were those "words of so sweet breath composed / As made the things more rich" (3.1.98–99), and by what other words and/or actions would he subsequently "prove [himself] unkind" (101) to her whom, as he admits, he "did love . . . once" (115), words and/or actions that, as she admits, "made [her] believe so" (116)? We also want to know about Hamlet's words and actions before the time of the play—words and actions we never *see* during the play, which now prompt Ophelia to lament the "o'erthrow" of "The courtier's, soldier's, scholar's, eye, tongue, sword, / . . . The glass of fashion and the mold of form, / Th' observed of all observers" (150–54): what did she hear (and what did she do) when she "sucked the honey of his music vows" (156), and why does what she sees and hears now provoke such "woe . . . T' have seen what [she has] seen" (160–61)?[5]

We are moved to ask questions such as these about the past lives of Hamlet and Ophelia because we willingly believe that they have past lives and experiences prior to their first meeting in 3.1, indeed prior to the time of the play itself, because the play is full of references to those past lives. Laertes tells Ophelia that Hamlet has been "trifling of his favor" with her (1.3.5) and later warns her that "if he says he loves you," do not "list his songs, / Or lose your heart, or your chaste treasure chest open / To his unmastered importunity" (23, 29–30). Something of the same information comes up later in the same scene when Polonius tells Ophelia he has heard that Hamlet has "very oft of late / Given private time to [her], and [that she her]self / Have of [her] audience been more free and bounteous" (90–92). People have been talking it seems, or so we can imagine when Polonius tells her that "so 'tis put on me" (93).

We are also led to imagine that Hamlet has a past life—that he has been away at school in Wittenburg, for instance, with both Horatio ("what make you from Wittenberg, Horatio?" [1.2.164]) and Rosencrantz and Guildenstern ("my two schoolfellows" [3.4.202]); that he has heard the Player "speak . . . a speech once, but it was never acted, or if it was, not above once" (2.2.375–76); that there was "One speech in't [he] chiefly loved. . . . Aeneas' tale to Dido" (386–87) about Priam's slaughter, which he believes (mistakenly, it turns out) begins, "The rugged Pyrrhus, like th' Hyrcanian beast" (390). We learn from Ophelia herself (an eyewitness) of a presumably more recent offstage action, which took place when Hamlet surprised her in "[her] closet, / With his doublet all unbraced"—everything in that speech and the even more provocative one which follows it being an instance of Ophelia's "remembrances" (in words) of physical action not performed in *Hamlet* except in these words, which are all that we in the audience are "shown" of a scene whose significance Polonius takes to be "the very ecstasy of love" (101):

> took me by the wrist and held me hard.
> Then goes he to the length of all his arm,

And with his other hand thus o'er his brow
He falls to such perusal of my face
As a would draw it. Long stayed he so.
At last, a little shaking of mine arm
And thrice his head thus waving up and down,
He raised a sigh so piteous and profound
As it did seem to shatter all his bulk
And end his being. That done, he lets me go,
And with his head over his shoulder turned
He seemed to find his way without his eyes,
For out o' doors he went without their helps
And to the last bended their light on me. (2.1.86–99)

(In Olivier's 1948 film, Ophelia's memory speech becomes a complex visual/acoustic "performance" both of Ophelia's verbal account of what took place—she tells her story of this action to us only, Olivier having removed Polonius from the scene, we in the audience thus being the only ear/eyewitnesses to her speech—and of a visual "flashback" of the action described by these words. As the scene unfolds, we see Hamlet walking slowing toward Ophelia, taking her by the left wrist, holding her at arm's length then pulling her close, looking up, letting her go, walking slowly backward— still facing her—toward the open doorway: all of this physical action accompanied by Ophelia's voice-over narrative account of it. What Olivier shows us in this scene is not what Shakespeare's text means for us to "see"—Ophelia telling her father what happened elsewhere, prior to the moment of her actually telling it to him here; her words in this speech are all we in the audience watching the play are "shown" of that previous offstage action. Nor does what happens in Olivier's film version of the action that Ophelia describes represent what *actually* but invisibly, because it happened offstage, may have happened in Ophelia's closet: how Hamlet "took [her] by the wrist and held [her] hard," and so on. Although Shakespeare's language here does not "say" that Hamlet had sex with Ophelia in her closet, nor does Olivier's film "show" any such thing, the language in this speech is nonetheless strange. And the language is all we are "shown"—not physical action, no (other) eyewitnesses, just words that in recalling how Hamlet "took [her] . . . and held [her] hard," how "Long stayed he so . . . his head thus waiving up and down," how "He raised a sigh so piteous and profound/As it did seem to shatter all his bulk/And end his being" possibly point to what Lisa Jardine has called an "anxious account of . . . an erotic entanglement."[6])

So what then are those "remembrances" that Ophelia wants to "redeliver" to Hamlet? The performance history of *Hamlet* says they are physical—letters, flowers, pictures, and so on—something the actor playing Ophelia can hand to the actor playing Hamlet, thus something that we who are watching the play in the theater will be able to *see*. And such stage props certainly make good sense in a stage performance.[7] Consider for instance the props used by the Royal Shakespeare Company in staging this scene: in 1975 (directed by Buzz Goodbody) they were flowers and beads; in 1980 (directed by John Barton) letters; in 1984 (directed by Ron Daniels) a necklace; in 1992 (directed by Adrian Noble), a suitcase full of things (clothes?) that Hamlet throws open when Ophelia tells him that her father is "At home, my lord"; in 1997 (directed by Mathew Warchus), letters and locket.[8] What each of these productions does not show us is what happened when Hamlet first gave Ophelia whatever it is she now tries to give him back. What is more, in four of these productions the plural of "remembrances" has been made to stand for multiple objects, things Hamlet gave (or sent) to Ophelia over a period of time—a packet of letters, things in the suitcase, flowers and beads—so the presence of these visible stage props suggests not a single moment of time but an expanse of it: days? weeks? months?—we know only that something has been happening between Hamlet and Ophelia for some time. And since there is nothing in the play about any of this, we do not know where they met or when, how often or what they did together: exchange glances? words? these gifts? was there more? physical contact perhaps? were they lovers? And if they were lovers, as one recent film version implies (Kenneth Branagh shows us Hamlet and Ophelia in bed together), is it not also possible that Ophelia is pregnant?

The point is that Shakespeare says nothing about any of this. All we know for sure is what we see with our eyes—and even such things are subject to interpretation: *did you see what I just saw?* And Shakespeare, in any case, doesn't show that scene in Ophelia's bedroom, where some kind of "erotic entanglement," as Lisa Jardine calls it, *might* have happened; "shows" us only in words that *might* suggest that such an intimate encounter has, possibly, taken place. All he gives us is language, and what we only hear about is *always* uncertain, not knowable: Hamlet's and Ophelia's past lives *are* completely invisible to the play's spectators, able only to be imagined, wondered about. As such, while it is *not* possible to "prove" that Ophelia is pregnant or that Hamlet and Ophelia have had sex (it is likely to raise eyebrows even to think such things[9]), the play itself, by withholding information, invites us to ask what it was that has "really" happened offstage between them.

Take for example the possibility of sexual innuendo in the exchange between Hamlet and Ophelia in *The Mousetrap* scene (what I am about to point out will, once again, hardly be noticed by an audience in the theater, not because it is not important but because the words race by too quickly, far too persuasively to our ears, for us to wonder about whatever meaning might be "concealed" in the words we are hearing). Hamlet interrupts the "To be or not to be" speech in line 88, announcing to the audience what he has just seen—"— Soft you now, / The fair Ophelia!"—which acts as a kind of stage direction signaling a shift from the private world of the soliloquy, in which "enterprises of great pitch and moment/With this regard their currents turn awry/And lose the name of action" (86–88), to present and public stage action. Although "Soft" refers here to the volume of Hamlet's speaking voice (he is telling himself to turn down the sound, stop speaking) and "you" to the speaker who delivers this line, both "soft" and "you" may also be understood in reference to Ophelia herself, who is being addressed here in the second person "you" and whose body is physically "soft[er]" than his.

When Hamlet moves from the name "Ophelia" to "Nymph" (here also used as a name), he suggests not only one of those semi-divine beings imagined as beautiful maidens inhabiting the sea, rivers, fountains, hills, woods, or trees—and, by extension, a beautiful young woman—but also a potentially sexual bride.[11] And do we also hear in what follows "Nymph"—"in thy orisons/Be all my sins remembered" (89–90), which places "thy orisons" in phonetic, grammatical, and ideational relation to "my sins"—the words "orifaces" and "sons"—and in such a momentary *mis*-hearing see six million of Hamlet's "sins" wriggling upstream to where one of them will be "remembered" as Hamlet's child? (No, we do *not* hear any such thing—my "wanton ingenuity" has taken hold of my senses, it seems; so please, forgive me, and bear with me while I continue what might appear to be a preposterous reading of this passage, which everyone by now knows so well, having heard it in the theater and read it on the page so many times.)

Ophelia's line, "Good my lord,/How does your honor for this many a day?", suggests that a certain amount of time has elapsed since he last saw her and she him. (Recalling her speech to Polonius in 2.1, perhaps they last met while she was sewing in her closet.) She seems to be toying with him here—"your honor" not only a form of address to a judge but also suggesting a woman's sexual honor[12]—a sense Hamlet plays on in the following ten lines: "Ha, ha! Are you honest? . . . That if you be honest and fair, your honesty should admit no discourse to your beauty. . . . for the power of beauty will sooner transform honesty from what it is to a bawd than the force of honesty can translate beauty into his likeness" (103–13).

Hamlet's reply to Ophelia's question ("I humbly thank you, well" [92]), which seems innocent enough at first hearing, may also suggest the potentially sexual meaning of "well" as female sex organ that Shakespeare seems to intend elsewhere.[13]

Ophelia's next speech also appears to be straightforward enough, acting as a kind of stage direction for the actress who plays Ophelia to do something with whatever "remembrances" she is holding in her hand. (At this point in Olivier's film of *Hamlet*, Jean Simmons pulls something—a necklace?—from the bosom of her white nightgownlike dress, holds it in her palm as she and Hamlet speak for the next ten lines, then places it on a stone table beside her at the line "There, my lord" [102].) But the echo in "redeliver" of these "remembrances" is anything but straightforward in a passage whose sexual innuendo is so well known, "deliver" often enough used by Shakespeare to mean "to bear a child"—particularly pertinent to the sense of "remembrances" (seed, child) I am thinking about here.[14] There may also be a buried sexual suggestion in the doubling of "longèd long," which here points toward offstage action we do not see ("longèd" being Ophelia's desire to return these "remembrances," "long" the amount of time she has had this desire), a sense that Shakespeare may also suggest in Gertrude's speech on Ophelia's death ("long purples, / That liberal shepherds give a grosser name, / But our cold maids do dead-men's-fingers call them" [4.7.167–69]).

Hamlet's "No, not I, / I never gave you aught" (95–96)—in which the twinning of one pair of connective, nearly identical monosyllables ("No" is echoed in the idea if not sound of "not," whose sound and idea are both later echoed in "aught") followed by a second pair of exactly identical monosyllables ("I," / "I") coupled with a fourfold reiteration of the negative ("No," "not," "never," "aught") points to action prior to the action that is taking place onstage[15]—amounts to an assertion of innocence in response to her assertion of his previous action, since Ophelia's "remembrances *of yours*" implies that Hamlet has at some point given these "remembrances of [his]" to her. (*If* Hamlet knows Ophelia is pregnant—conjecture of course, because Shakespeare gives no real "evidence" in *Hamlet* that she might be—he is the second person in the play to know it, Ophelia being the first. But others will know soon enough, and *if* he now means to separate himself from this woman who, he believes, has been enlisted to trap him, his "No, not I, I never gave you aught" may be read as his attempt to put the blame of paternity on someone else's loins.)

Countering Hamlet's protest of innocence, Ophelia's next speech potentially "pictures," in graphic detail, the physical act of having sex that led to her present condition: "My honored lord, you know right well you did,/And with them words of so sweet breath composed/As made the things more rich./Their perfume lost" (97–99). While rich with possible sexual overtones—"well" and "things" suggesting the female and male sex organs, "you did" the sexual act, "breath" Hamlet's words and sighs in the act of love-making and, taking it also to mean "spirit,"[16] his sperm or seed, whose viscous texture she here calls both "sweet" and "rich," and whose smell ("perfume") and maybe also taste ("sweet") has been lost—the speech also says exactly what it seems to say ("you know you gave me these things, you said some sweet things when you gave them") and thus calls no attention to such potential of "surplus meaning" concealed in these salient but, in the theater at least, easily missed overtones.

In the exchange of four quick questions that follow in lines 103–6—

> HAMLET Ha, ha! Are you honest?
> OPHELIA My lord?
> HAMLET Are you fair?

OPHELIA What means your lordship?

—we are invited to move rapidly back and forth between the previous offstage action implied by Hamlet's questions, which suggest he knows Ophelia is deceiving him in her complicity with whomever is now hidden onstage watching this present action, and Ophelia's previous (unseen) offstage action, which his questions suggest has taken place. Asking us to shift between previous and present offstage and onstage action, these lines also invite us to notice the complexity of the equation that Hamlet draws between "honest" and "fair," which connects the idea of honesty both to Ophelia's sexual honor and to her physical beauty ("fair[ness]") which Hamlet has already acknowledged in this scene ("Soft you now, / The fair Ophelia").

Hamlet continues to talk about the relationship between honesty and beauty in lines 107–15, which continue to suggest the idea of both sexual relations and the offspring they might produce:

> HAMLET That if you be honest and fair, your honesty
> should admit no discourse to your beauty.
> OPHELIA Could beauty, my lord, have better commerce
> than with honesty?
> HAMLET Ay, truly; for the power of beauty will sooner
> transform honesty from what it is to a bawd than
> the force of honesty can translate beauty into his
> likeness. This was sometime a paradox, but now
> the time gives it proof. I did love you once.

As "proof" of Ophelia's "[dis]honesty," Hamlet claims that the "beauty" of women who are truly virtuous "should admit no discourse"—meaning here "familiar intercourse, familiarity with a subject,"[17] especially in this context sexual familiarity/intercourse— "to their beauty." The "beauty" of "honest" women "should" be unassailable, he argues, except that the body's appetite for physical pleasure is more powerful than the mind's ability to curb that appetite by practicing abstinence or celibacy, which "honesty," in the moral sense that Hamlet here uses it, should set into motion: lust will "transform" an "honest" woman into a "bawd" sooner than "honesty can translate beauty into his likeness"—as a father's image is reproduced in his child—because her desire for the pleasures of the flesh outweighs whatever restraint her mind may attempt to exercise against it.

The end of Hamlet's speech ("This was sometime a paradox, but now the time gives it proof. I did love you once.") followed by Ophelia's "Indeed, my lord, you made me believe so" (114–16) continues a train of possible sexual innuendo along the same track. His "paradox" posits a contest between (Hamlet's) "honesty" and (Ophelia's) "beauty"—one in which the two participants wage the kind of battle of wills that Hamlet at least seems to be waging here in words. But that contest took place somewhere in the past and elsewhere (offstage), two lovers' "beauty" (or lust) winning out over the restraining judgment of their "honesty," and now the effect of such a fall from innocence is *perhaps* making itself evident ("now the time gives it proof") in Ophelia's soon noticeably rounded belly. In view of such a reading of the scene as I am thinking about, Hamlet's "I did love you once" may be a confession not only that he was once in love with Ophelia but that he once made love to her, as Ophelia's reply ("Indeed, my lord, you made me believe so") may also perhaps suggest. (This reading is of course far fetched, since if Hamlet had made love to Ophelia she most certainly would have known it; at the same time, it points to the fact that the undelivered potential of sexually charged language in this scene is itself equally far fetched—much of it equally unnoticed—and nonetheless all the more effective for that reason.) If Hamlet "made" Ophelia in a sexual sense (a sense Shakespeare plays on elsewhere,[18] in her songs of 4.5 for instance), he becomes one of the ways she was "made [to] believe" he was in love with her, a belief she laments the loss of in 4.5 as much as anything.

Hamlet's speech in lines 117–19 continues the case of "honesty" against "beauty," translated here into "virtue" and "our old stock," which cannot be "inoculate[d]" against a susceptibility to sexual desire:

You should not have believed me, for virtue cannot so inoculate our old stock but we shall relish of it. I loved you not.

In addition to the phallic suggestion in "our old stock" (the male root or stem, which virtue cannot in a horticultural sense "inoculate" against its appetite for lust), the sense Hamlet means it to convey here (lineage, our genealogical tree[19]) also suggests a passing along of one's genetic code—a meaning relevant in this context, in which the man may be understood to be speaking to the mother-to-be of his unborn child about who and what the child will turn out to be.[20]

And so Hamlet gets to his "Get thee to a nunnery" tirade, its fury possibly unleashed at his thought of an unborn child (whom he calls a "sinner") born of this "breeder" upon whom he spills his venom in lines 121–30:

Get thee to a nunnery. Why would'st thou be a breeder of sinners? I am myself indifferent honest, but yet I could accuse me of such things that it were better my mother had not borne me: I am very proud, revengeful, ambitious, with more offenses at my beck than I have thoughts to put them in, imagination to give them shape, or time to act them in. What should such fellows as I do crawling between earth and heaven? We are arrant knaves all; believe none of us. Go thy ways to a nunnery. Where's your father?

Hamlet's use of "nunnery" both as sanctuary for women who want nothing physical to do with men and also as a place whose purpose is to permit, indeed to enable, men to have physical contact with woman in exchange for money (contact that may well result in pregnancy) sets the stage for a virtually non-stop onslaught of loaded references both to that contact (or its absence) and its potential outcome.[21] Hamlet thinks about his own birth in "better my mother had not borne me" (123–24), for example, and gestation itself in "imagination to give them shape" (126–27). He also imagines himself as a baby "crawling between earth and heaven" (128); wants Ophelia to be "chaste as ice, as pure as snow" (136); is disillusioned by the fact that, in giving birth to men, women make "monsters . . . of them" (139–40), that "God hath given you one face, and you make yourselves another" (143–44), that women "jig . . . amble, and . . . lisp" (144); that women (anti-Adam and also baby-talking) "nickname God's creatures and make your wantonness your ignorance" (144–45); then proclaims against all further licensed physical contact between men and women ("I say we shall have no more marriages" [147]), after which he leaves the stage.

Nor, though Hamlet has now disappeared from our sight, is this the end of his presence in this scene, for Ophelia immediately begins to "remember" him for us, as he used to be, this verbal picture making his physical absence into a literal presence:

> O, what a noble mind is here o'erthrown!
> The courtier's, soldier's, scholar's, eye, tongue, sword,
> Th' expectancy and rose of the fair state,
> The glass of fashion and the mold of form,
> Th' observed of all observers, quite, quite down!
> And I, of ladies most deject and wretched,
> That sucked the honey of his music vows,
> Now see that noble and most sovereign reason
> Like sweet bells jangled, out of time and harsh,
> That unmatched form and feature of blown youth
> Blasted with ecstasy. O, woe is me
> T' have seen what I have seen, see what I see.
>   (150–61)

And once again, while Ophelia clearly means exactly what she is saying here ("O . . . [this is not the Hamlet I once knew] . . . woe is me"), the language of her speech is also informed by the "surplus meaning" of various "buried," not-likely-to-be-noticed-in-the-theater, suggestions of sex: the phallic potential of "tongue" and "sword" for example; the idea of the male passing his lineage on by means of his seed in "mold of form"; the graphic re-enactment of what seems to have been an act of love-making, one in which Ophelia had "sucked the honey of [Hamlet's] music vows" and saw his "blown youth"—in the moment of sexual climax?—"Blasted with ecstasy."

And so it is with a certain irony that Shakespeare has Claudius say, when he reappears onstage, "Love? his affections do not that way tend." On the contrary, although it is only "circumstantial evidence," the verbal performance of offstage action in *Hamlet* makes it possible to imagine that Hamlet and Ophelia have been not only platonic lovers but physical ones, and that as a result of this physically unperformed (but verbally suggested) action she may be pregnant with his child. I cannot as I say ever "prove" it, since things that happen offstage cannot ever be known—can only be speculated about, are therefore always uncertain, subject to one's interpretation of the words (which do *not* "show" such things, so we never actually *see* them, only *hear* of them, ear rather than eye) the play uses to suggest them. Meanwhile, I would once again send the reader who might still not have been persuaded "[t]' have seen what I have seen, see what I see," as Ophelia puts it in this scene, to the "country matters" passage in 3.2, whose language suggests the easy manner of sexual banter between lovers:

> HAMLET Lady, shall I lie in your lap?
> OPHELIA No, my Lord.
> [HAMLET I mean, my head upon your lap?
> OPHELIA Ay, my lord.]

HAMLET Do you think I mean country matters?
OPHELIA I think nothing, my lord.
HAMLET That's a fair thought to lie between maids'
　　legs.
OPHELIA What is, my lord?
HAMLET Nothing.
　. . .
OPHELIA You are keen, my lord, you are keen.
HAMLET It would cost you a groaning to take off mine
　　edge.　　　　　　　　　　　　(110–16, 244–46)

And if that is not enough, then also to Ophelia's "mad" songs in 4.5, where the multiple sexual innuendoes of the play's language—"cockle hat and staff" (25), the man who "rose" (52) and "Let in the maid, that out a maid / Never departed more" (54–55), the "Young men [who] will do't if they come to't. / By Cock, they are to blame" (60–61), the maid who says "Before you tumbled me, / You promised me to wed" and the man who replies "So would I 'a' done, by yonder sun, / And thou hadst not come to my bed" (62–63, 65–66), the maid who says "Bonny sweet Robin is all my joy"[22] (181)—will again suggest that, in Shakespeare's mind at least, something may have happened offstage (in Ophelia's closet perhaps) between Hamlet and Ophelia.

Let me move forward now to Hamlet's mother's bedroom, the closet scene itself. It is here that Hamlet—having stabbed Polonius (who stands "Behind the arras . . . To hear the process . . . o'erhear / The speech" [3.3.28–29, 32–33][23]) and seen the ghost of his father (whom his mother does not see) dressed not in armor but only "his nightgown," according to the stage direction in the First Quarto[24]—urges his mother to have no more sex with her second husband, Hamlet's uncle, whose actions in murdering his father and having sex with his mother "In the rank sweat of an enseamèd bed, / Stewed in corruption, honeying and making

love / Over the nasty sty—" (3.4.93–95), have become so offensive
to him. Olivier's *Hamlet* cuts this scene entirely, so let me for a
moment imagine it: Hamlet directly in front of Gertrude, holding her by the wrist, looking her straight in the eye—all of these
physical actions being performed onstage as he himself "performs"
(in the words of his speech) something that does not happen on
the stage of *Hamlet* except in words—these words, in response to
Gertrude's question, "What shall I do?":

> Not this, by no means, that I bid you do:
> Let the bloat king tempt you again to bed,
> Pinch wanton on your cheek, call you his mouse,
> And let him, for a pair of reechy kisses,
> Or paddling in your neck with his damned fingers,
> Make you to ravel all this matter out,
> That I essentially am not in madness,
> But mad in craft. (3.4.181–88)

Like Ophelia's speech to her father telling him how Hamlet came
into her closet "with his doublet all unbraced," Hamlet's speech
here pictures something that is not performed physically in the
play, these two rhymelike closet speeches being parallel but also
mirror opposites of one another. Each one invites us to imagine
something that does not take place onstage except in words—words
that present an image first of previous offstage action, then of action to come (action that Hamlet believes has happened previously
and will, he fears, if his mother does what he here bids her not to
do, happen again); one in which a daughter *appears* to tell her father that Hamlet has talked with her, the other in which a son *appears* to tell his mother not to have sex with her husband; one that
perhaps "shows" Hamlet having sex with the female speaker, who
describes that action, the other that "shows" his uncle having sex
with the female listener, who hears him describe in explicit detail
the action he imagines has taken place before and will take place

again—action that Hamlet is both revolted by and, as Freudian readings argue, may subconsciously wish to perform.[25]

Before looking at the speech, let me say again that the effects I am about to describe will not ever be noticed by someone in the theater watching and listening to a performance of the play. Take for example the multiplicity of potential echoes and meanings—also mistaken meanings, misreadings—set into motion by Hamlet's answer to his mother's question, "What shall I do?": "Not this, by no means, that I bid you do." Gertrude's question at the end of line 180 ends with "I do," which rhymes phonetically and also ideationally with Hamlet's answer at the end of line 181, "you do"—Hamlet's "do" seemingly identical to his mother's "do" (in fact it is not); Hamlet's second person "you" (which repeats the sound in his next word, "do") referring to the same person as his mother's first person "I," whose sound it does not echo—"I" at this moment both equal and not equal to "you." Hamlet's "you" (meaning Gertrude, whom she refers to in the preceding line's "I do") is itself preceded by his own first person "I," which operates in a four-part pronoun-verb-pronoun-verb series of words ("I bid you do") in which the first-person speaker orders the second-person listener to "do" something—take some action, perform some command—exactly what he does not yet say. Thus asking his mother to "do" (something), the grammatical structure of Hamlet's statement—"I" (subject) "bid" (verb) "you" (object, who is being asked to become the subject who will "do" something) "do" (verb, whose not yet disclosed action will be, if Hamlet has his way with her, whatever it is that he is about to ask his mother to "do")— literally "performs" the cause-and-effect sequence of subject-verb actions that it commands: "I [Hamlet] bid [and then, as a result] you [Gertrude] do."

Notice as well this sound effect we are not likely to hear, not consciously at least, in a stage performance of *Hamlet*: the acoustic echo at the end of line 187—"Not this, by no means, that *I bid you do*"—of the Ghost's farewell to Hamlet at 1.5.91 (*"Adieu, adieu, adieu"*) which itself echoes the sound, but not sense, of the last two words in the second line of Hamlet's first soliloquy—"O that this too too sullied flesh would melt, / Thaw, and resolve itself into *a dew*" (1.2.129–30). Although we don't notice effects like this in the theater nor in any but the closest of readings, they are I say again more important than noticed effects because they "show" us that we do *not* "see" what isn't performed physically in the play—things like Hamlet having sex with Ophelia, his fantasy of his mother having sex with his uncle; that it doesn't matter that we don't notice (indeed, that it is aesthetically crucial that we do *not* notice); and that what isn't noticed or "seen" because it isn't shown (only talked about) is uncertain, can't ever be known for sure, is always subject to speculation and conjecture, physical "evidence" (which is here "missing," not "shown") always in the end necessary to "show" what "really" happened, set the record straight.

Hamlet's command that his mother "do:" (something) would appear to lead to an account of whatever it is that the following words will ask her to "do: / Let the bloat king tempt you again to bed." That is not what Hamlet wants, or "means" to say, of course, since the words "I bid you do" themselves follow a six-word phrase ("Not this, by no means, that") whose meaning, though it seems clear enough and will always be understood by anyone in the audience to *be* clear, is anything but clear. For one thing, the effect of the double negative ("Not . . . no") is both to make the negative command more emphatic (common in Elizabethan usage) *and* to contradict what a single negative would claim—as in the phrase "I don't not understand you," which we understand to mean "I understand you." For another, the demonstrative pronoun "this," which stands for the action Hamlet is about to disclose to his mother, leads as the line continues to the relative pronoun "that" (here standing for an ellipsis, "that which") whose complex syntactic and semantic relation to "this" (i.e., "this" . . . [action, which he is about to name, both is and is not the same as] . . . "that" [action]), though it appears to be, and is, perfectly clear is anything but straightforward.[26]

Hamlet begins to tell his mother what he "by no means" wants her to "do" in the line 183, "Let the bloat king tempt you again to bed," which is ordered phonetically by a pattern of short *e* sounds in which the verb ("Let . . . tempt") is linked to the object of the preposition ("bed"), while the adverb ("again") suggests that the action that Hamlet imagines will take place there—sex between his mother and his uncle—and that, picturing it graphically in words here, he appears to want not to take place, has already taken place at least once (probably many times) and, he imagines, may well take place again.[27] This sentence's implied but missing subject ("you"), whose imperative verb ("Let . . . tempt") leads to a grammatical object ("the bloat king"—"bloat" possibly suggesting Hamlet's uncle's enlarged member) that becomes the subject who performs the action that Hamlet is imagining here—the aggressor in Hamlet's sexual fantasy (Hamlet's "mighty opposite"[28]) but also Hamlet himself, as Gertrude's line in the final scene also suggests ("He's fat and scant of breath" [5.2.270])—"you" is also the line's grammatical object, the object of both the "bloat king['s]" and Hamlet's desire.

In the following line, "Pinch wanton on your cheek, call you his mouse," Hamlet's verbal picture of the action that will take place (and, as he imagines, has already taken place) presumably in the same bedroom as the speech now being performed onstage, moves from a wide angle camera shot to a close-up, one that includes both physical action (which can be seen) and sound (which can be heard). Whereas the action of the preceding line leaves much to our imagination (just how might this "bloat king" tempt his wife

into bed?), Hamlet (Ophelia's lover? at least in these lines something of a Don Juan) now reveals his own trade secrets: "Pinch
wanton on [the woman's] cheek, call [her] his mouse." Notice
what we do not notice in the theater: the mental gymnastics by
which "your cheek" (a metonymy for Hamlet's mother) becomes
"his mouse" (his wanton uncle's wanton sex toy[29]); how the *ch*
sound of "Pinch" echoed in "cheek" also pulls those two words
together, one the verb of action, one the object on which that action takes place—his mother's cheek thus becoming both present
(visible onstage during this speech) and absent (the offstage site
where the sexual encounter Hamlet imagines will supposedly take
place); how what Hamlet supposes his uncle will call his mother
("his mouse") also echoes what Hamlet called his play within the
play (*"The Mousetrap"*), thereby also linking the lover's action in
Hamlet's bedroom fantasy to Hamlet's own previous action in the
play.

   As Hamlet's speech continues, "And let him, for a pair of reechy
kisses" repeats the verb "Let" of two lines before—the pattern
"Let . . . And Let" suggesting the ongoing, continuous offstage action that Hamlet's words now seem almost obsessively to be imagining, and also condenses the adjective-plus-noun phrase "bloat
king" to one blunt pronoun, "him." But whereas line 182 supplied an object for its "bloat king" to act upon ("tempt *you* again to
bed"), this line withholds that object, giving in its place an image,
embedded in the prepositional phrase "for a pair of reechy kisses,"
whose "view" of that action, which Hamlet here imagines as being
performed by the male aggressor upon the (willing) female object
of his desire, gives us a close-up "show" of his disgust. And what
exactly are these "reechy kisses," one might ask, since they are
never actually performed onstage except in these words, though
the sound of "reechy kisses" seems to suggest the physical act of
lips placed on a cheek (as in *Othello* 4.1.71, "To lip a wanton"), are

"imagined" only in Hamlet's words here, whose acoustic "action" works to make that physically unperformed action as graphically "visible" as possible.[30]

The next line, "Or paddling in your neck with his damned fingers," continues to withhold the verb that the previous line's syntax suggests will follow, as it did in the pattern that it echoes two lines before ("Let the bloat king *tempt*," "And let him . . . [*verb*]"), presenting instead what proves to be this speech's final, most emotionally explosive image of imagined sexual action. Hamlet's vision of Claudius "paddling" not on but "in" Gertrude's neck makes the action being described more tactile: these fingers not only touch "your neck," they press into it, denting it with the pressure they apply.[31] The echo of "your cheek" in "your neck" moves the action of Claudius's fingers touching Gertrude to a more intimate part of her body ("your neck" could also be read as vaginal, since then his fingers would certainly be "in" it), closer to those parts of it that are, or may be, still clothed, felt but not seen. Similarly, the echo of "his mouse" in "his damned fingers" shifts our focus of attention from the object of Claudius's (and, in this speech at least, Hamlet's) desire to the part of his body now making its way (groping) toward it.

After Hamlet's vision of these "fingers" (the word will be echoed in Gertrude's speech on Ophelia's death, where she refers to the name that "liberal shepherds" give to the flowers Ophelia weaves into her garland as "dead-men's-fingers"), the close-up view of the sexual encounter that Hamlet imagines will take place in this same bedroom seems to dissolve, turning from this literal vision of offstage action to an ongoing concern of the play's plot: "Make you to ravel all this matter out / That I essentially am not in madness, / But mad in craft." What happens at the end of the sentence manages both to keep the focus on an offstage action Hamlet believes will take place between Claudius and Gertrude (Hamlet has persuaded her to tell his uncle that he, Hamlet, is not mad). At the same time, in finally supplying the second half of the predicate begun two lines before in "And let him," "Make you" momentarily continues to imagine the imagined sexual action that has been the focus of Hamlet's speech ("Let him . . . Make you"), and also to shift that focus back to what is now happening onstage (Hamlet's behavior shows that he is crafty—or, depending on how one reads it, indeed mad). Thus we are made witness to action that takes place simultaneously—in this moment at least—both on- and offstage: action that has happened before (Hamlet imagines his mother and uncle have had sex); action that will happen in the future (Hamlet imagines his mother will have sex unless she does something to prevent it); action that happens in the present (in this "performance," in Hamlet's words, of sex between his mother and his uncle—a "performance" of the madness, or "mad[ness] in craft," that "imagines" it).

In conclusion, let me return to a statement from A. C. Bradley's *Shakespearean Tragedy*, published just over one hundred years ago: "This is the position in which I find myself in regard to Hamlet's love for Ophelia. I am unable to arrive at a conviction as to the meaning of some of his words and deeds, and I question whether from the mere text of the play a sure interpretation of them can be drawn."[32] Bradley's skepticism here, in light of what he calls "some of his words and deeds," shows an appropriate direction to take in our response to the play at this point. Because Shakespeare chose to present certain key events in the play only verbally, we are never going to know for sure what exactly "happened" in it—not only what is not performed physically onstage (what we do not see, what we hear about only in words) but what the words and actions performed onstage really meant to Shakespeare, to his audience, or for that matter mean to us now. As with that of van Eyck's

Arnolfini portrait, the play's "perennial fascination" has everything to do with uncertainty, enigma, mystery, doubt: the unknowableness of Hamlet's "undiscovered country, from whose bourn no traveler returns" (3.1.79–80); an also unseeable, thus fascinating, unknowableness of what "happened" in Ophelia's closet; what the "remembrances [she has] longèd long to redeliver" to Hamlet might be; how those two "reechy kisses" that Hamlet imagines Claudius giving to Gertrude might look or feel or be received. We are left in the dark so to speak, left to speculate about what Shakespeare leaves out of the play, which is why we keep coming back to it, wanting more.

Afterword
"Who's There?" (II):
Offstage Shakespeare

"Who's there?" Barnardo asks at the beginning of *Hamlet*, addressing Francisco, who replies, "Nay, answer me. Stand and unfold yourself." Taking that question as my starting point, I want to give the line not to the guard on the castle walls but to the reader of Shakespeare's plays, the reader who asks of those plays, Who's there? Who was Shakespeare? Who wrote Shakespeare's plays?

Most of us, though by no means all, believe that the evidence leads to William Shakespeare of Stratford (1564–1616): son of John Shakespeare and Mary Arden (both of Stratford), the husband of Anne Hathaway and father of Susanna and the two twins, Judith and Hamnet, whose death at the age of eleven in 1596 may still have been on his mind when he wrote *Hamlet* (entered in the Stationers' Register in July of 1602), as possibly was the death of his father (1601). All of this and more is well known and available to anybody who wants to know more about the man who wrote the plays attributed to Shakespeare—the man whose image looks out at readers from the title page of the First Folio, identified as the "Figure that thou here seest" in Jonson's frontispiece "To the Reader," which goes on to make the distinction between Shakespeare's body ("His face," which can be seen) and his mind ("his wit," which cannot) and concludes by asking that we read Shakespeare's text not to discover his body but his mind, its words: "Reader, looke/Not on his Picture, but his Booke."[1]

In asking as Barnardo does "Who's there?" I am interested here not in the biographical identity of the man who wrote Shakespeare's plays but in the plain, indeed obvious fact that the author is now "missing," has literally disappeared into the text of *Hamlet*, which "echoes" who he was (and thus bestows on him an immortality he imagines in the sonnets) but at the same time fails to make him physically present, to recall him back from that "undiscovered country," as Hamlet puts it, "from whose bourn/No traveler returns" (3.1.79–80). And it is this long deceased, absent ("offstage") man William Shakespeare—whose ghostly presence haunts his plays, especially of course *Hamlet*, its "ghostlier demarcations, keener sounds" pointing to the offstage originary presence of an author behind the words—who cannot be seen.[2] These words are all we have to show us who he was or what he thought about or felt or had to say for himself: words that sometimes point (if only obliquely) to the fact, or at least the possibility, of his presence— but also absence—in them; that continue to be sayable (and thus hearable) whenever they are performed, although the person who wrote them is no longer now seeable. It is this "disappearance"— of Shakespeare the physical person into words—that I want to ask about here in relation to offstage action in *Hamlet*, which is itself also "missing," also physically absent, also represented in words that refer to things not performed physically onstage (are thus not seen). In both cases, the words we hear in performance, or read on the page, are the "echo" or "shadow" or "trace" of this "missing" (said-but-not-seen) person William Shakespeare and the "missing" (said-but-not-seen) action that his words "perform." And it is this absence both of Shakespeare and of the offstage action in *Hamlet* that I here want to acknowledge: an essential absence that forces us to imagine the missing parts or person based on the words the play uses to "perform" them; to formulate images in our minds, both of things not performed physically onstage and also of William Shakespeare the man (call him "Shakespeare") whose life, we assume, is connected to the works we attribute to him—whose words stand in place of someone who no longer exists, a person whose "I" is nothing, a blank, zero, but whose characters "represent" him verbally, punctuate his plays by asking of themselves and each other, "Who's there?"³

Wanting to know the man behind the text, the action not performed physically onstage, we instead find language: blank, oblique, evasive, impenetrable, the surface "I" embodies but will not explain. "What I believe, hear, feel is in my texts which say it," Edmund Jabès writes, *"sometimes without quite saying it."*⁴ This "I" whom "texts . . . say" is nothing: a one-dimensional vertical line, without depth or weight or mass, a presence that cannot be known except as the pronoun no one is standing behind—not "Shakespeare" the man, not some real person who speaks that "I."⁵ Speaking as if to articulate the impossibility of ever finding that nothing (the author who is not there, the figure of "Shakespeare" embedded within his text), Lear's "Nothing will come of nothing" (1.1.89) suggests how truly "blank," as Kent says, "thine eye/[I]" (1.1.158) is: no one there but the body of words "I" informs. What the Fool says to Lear aims as well at the absence of "Shakespeare" that his words represent: "thou art an O without a figure . . . thou art nothing" (1.4.176–78). And if, as Gloucester says to his bastard son Edgar, "The quality of nothing hath not such need to hide itself" (1.2.34–35), the nothing that is "Shakespeare"'s "I" is nonetheless hidden in the text whose body is not his but one made of his words: the text whose "face" or surface (language) both holds and witholds "Shakespeare"'s body—how it looks, what we see when we see or hear him in the room, walking or talking, the absent physical (offstage) presence behind the words.

If a play by "Shakespeare" is, in literal terms, "Shakespeare"'s body (face), it also demonstrates what its characters consistently find—that one's face is not an index to one's mind. "Honest Iago"'s face is not, or, as he puts it, "I am not what I am" (*Othello*, 1.1.64). "Shakespeare" explores the relationship between the person and his name, written as proper noun or pronoun, the subject "I" or the person "I" stands for, in terms presented as reciprocals or negatives of one another. "Were I the Moor, I would not be Iago" (1.1.56), Iago tells Roderigo; "Not I; I must be found" (1.2.30), Othello says in response to Iago's warning that he hide himself from his father-in-law. In plays performed by actors playing characters who sometimes take on other roles (a male actor who plays Rosalind plays Ganymede playing Rosalind) the one who speaks or acts is often not the one who seems to speak or act. "I am not what I am" Viola says in *Twelfth Night* (3.1.140), a line repeated by Iago, whom she anticipates in other words when she says, "I am not that I play" (1.5.177). Desdemona voices a similar idea when she says "My lord is not my lord" (3.4.123), then articulates even more succinctly the absent presence of "Shakespeare," whose "I" stands for both author and character alike, when she says, in response to Emilia's question as to who has assaulted her, "Nobody—I myself" (5.2.125). The question she addresses to Iago, "Am I that name, Iago" (4.2.118); Angelo's question to himself ("I" addressed here as "you"), "What art thou, Angelo?" (*Measure for Measure* 2.2.172); Edgar's sense that "Edgar I nothing am" (2.3.21); Lear's own discovery and question when he says, "This is not Lear. . . . Who is it that can tell me who I am?" to which the Fool replies, "Lear's shadow" (1.4.210–15); Richard's punning "Ay, no; no, ay; for I must nothing be" (4.1.201); Duncan asking Malcolm, "What bloody man is that?" (1.2.1)—which becomes *Macbeth's* question given that Macbeth, who first murders his kinsman, king, and guest, then turns to a string of serial killings that leaves his country in ruins, is the play's most "bloody man": the fact of lines like these returns us to Barnardo's "Who's there?" by which I mean again to ask, Who was "Shakespeare"?

As readers, we feel compelled to know the man himself, embodied in a text whose performance shows the writing subject— "Shakespeare"—encountering a number of other subjects—his characters, readers, members of the audience. How are we to know that person whose eye/"I" looks out from the title page of the First Folio, whose words fill pages? We continue to ask these questions, wanting to know (as if "personally") the author himself, as if in that face-to-face immediacy of relation one will understand what the text (therefore its maker) is saying. We want to know, as Foucault writes, "where [the text] come[s] from, who wrote it, when, under what circumstances, or beginning with what design,"[6] because the answers to such questions will show us, we assume, what the text itself means. We ask such questions because we think that, by tracing a text (its author's body in words) to someone who made it, we will be able to discover what the text always resists giving up: its significance, that set of instructions that tells us how to read (and also interpret) it. Confronted with simply the text by itself and wanting at that moment not only to make sense of it but to understand what "Shakespeare" meant for us to understand when he wrote it, we assume inevitably that "Shakespeare" is the key: both source of what we read (and want to understand) and end to which our understanding might, if we are attentive enough, lead us. As Barthes has famously, if now controversially, written,

The image of literature to be found in ordinary culture is tyrannically centered on the author, his person, his life, his tastes, his passions. . . . The *explanation* of a work is always sought in the man or woman who produced it, as if it were always in the end, through the more or less transparent allegory of the fiction, the voice of a single person, the *author* "confiding" in us.[7]

Unlocking the door to *The Turn of The Screw*, we think to say "This is what James meant." Seeing *Hamlet* performed onstage or reading it, we want to arrive at the same conclusion: this is what "Shakespeare" meant—by Hamlet's father's ghost, by Hamlet's delay, by Hamlet's turning against Ophelia and his mother, by the play *Hamlet* itself.[8]

Though we want to come to such conclusions, our impulse to "read" "Shakespeare" in *Hamlet* runs the risk of misreading (or simply missing) the text itself—its language, the body of words that embodies (even as it withholds) its author. As soon as its words reach the reader's eye or listener's ear, "Shakespeare" may be said to have disappeared. He is not present when the actor who plays Leontes says "even at this present,/Now while I speak this" (*The Winter's Tale* 1.2.191–92). Nor when Ferdinand cries to Prospero "Let me live here ever!" (*The Tempest* 4.1.122). Nor when the Duke confesses "I love the people,/But do not like to stage me to their eyes" (*Measure for Measure* 1.1.67–68). Or should I say he is not physically present, which is not to say that "Shakespeare" is not "here" whenever I read his words or hear them spoken—"here" verbally that is, as its offstage action is also "here" in the words *Hamlet* uses to "perform" it.

To paraphrase Jonson's "To the Reader," while there is no direct readable connection between the body of his text and "Shakespeare," no direct access through words to his body, "no art," as Duncan says, "To find the mind's construction in the face" (1.4.11–12), seeing his play performed onstage or reading it in a book does construct "Shakespeare": constructs him literally, in words, which also construct its missing offstage action—which like "Shakespeare" is sayable but unseeable. By which I mean again to suggest that while we are wrong to think we can ever discover "Shakespeare" in his plays—he is private, interior, signified by "I"—or the public body of his words, "Shakespeare" is in a real sense equal to his pronoun "I." We cannot unfold that "I" standing behind the text because that person is words, is himself missing. "[T]he writing subject cancels out the sign of his particular individuality," as Foucault says, "the mark of the writer is reduced to nothing more than the singularity of his absence."[9] Or as Hamlet explains it, "I have that within which passes show" (1.2.85), which is to say that "Shakespeare"'s body is never embodied in words— never, that is, except as "I."

None of this is news of course, since the New Critics formulated essentially the same argument in the 1940s.[10] "Shakespeare"'s "disappearance" into the language of his text, the transformation of that subject into words that resist leading us back to that person, means that his words (on the page or on the stage, there to be read or heard by the reader or listener), take on a life of their own, independent of the person who, in writing them, has given up all authority, has no power over either his words or the reader or listener who would interpret them. So too with the things that happen offstage in *Hamlet*, which, since they are not shown physically (cannot be seen) can only be imagined. What "really" happened in Hamlet's father's orchard? Or in Ophelia's closet? Or on the banks of the stream? Or on a Danish ship taking Hamlet to England? One can only speculate, because the play denies anything more than its words say, indeed refuses to "show" anything beyond what the Ghost says, what Ophelia says, what Gertrude says, what even Hamlet himself says. Likewise, we have no reason to think that we can ever "know" the author of *Hamlet*. Reading, like listening, becomes an act of relationship not between reader and "Shakespeare" but between the reader and the play—a text that does not express its author ("Shakespeare") but is an unfolding, multifaceted, constructed formation of the body whose bones and tissues and systems of material, thought, and feeling have been transformed into this identity made not of flesh but words. I read *Hamlet* to experience how the words of such a play make meanings of (and on) their own; where such meanings lie; what they might indeed be. I know that all my "answers" to these speculations will always be provisional (because the play resists giving any definitive "answers") and also subject to revision by future readers and audiences, who will bring the background of their own cultural moment to bear on reading and listening to what *Hamlet*'s words "say."

If *Hamlet* resists one's desire to discover the subject behind it and its meanings—if, as Barthes writes, "Writing is the destruction of every voice, of every point of origin . . . that neutral, composite, oblique space where our subject slips away, the negative where all identity is lost, starting with the very identity of the body writing"[11]—we must also ask whether the play is nonetheless still concerned with projecting and masking the identity of the man who wrote it: in other words, do these works represent the subjectivity of that person whose inward psychic, emotional, and thinking self we identify by the name "Shakespeare"?[12] It may be useful to think about "Shakespeare," who is in this regard the emblem of all writers, in light of what Keats once called "Shakespeare"'s "*Negative Capability*, that is, when a man is capable of being in uncertainties, Mysteries, doubts, without any irritable reaching after fact and reason."[13] If we see "Negative Capability" as "Shakespeare"'s power to dissolve himself into words (and dissolve the action not performed onstage in his play into words), invert that self's "positive" into its "negative" so to speak, and if we understand this dissolution of the person in light of an oblique (negative) space that Barthes claims constitutes writing, we will construct a way of reading that asks us to see the text as a surface that represents the unrepresented—and unrepresentatable—inward self of "Shakespeare," whose privacy, secrecy, and interiority his plays' surfaces inscribe. What is inside "Shakespeare" (his private self, his "I") is signified by what is outside (the written, "public" body of the text): writing is, to paraphrase Harry Berger, Jr., a task of inscribing the soul on the body, inside on the outside.[14] But even though we want to believe that the image of "Shakespeare"'s face that appears on the title page of the First Folio is the index of his mind, and that the writing that follows that image can "show" us the person who cannot be known, and that the offstage action that *Hamlet*'s words "show" can also be seen and known, "something more than meets the eye is always," as Berger, Jr. says, "something more than meets the eye."

That which is more is the unseen—unseeable—"Shakespeare," whose presence can be felt but not touched; whose plays keep taking up questions of identity (who is Hamlet, the Moor, Lear, Macbeth, Antony, Prospero? who is Ophelia, Gertrude, Rosalind, Viola, Desdemona, Cordelia, Lady Macbeth, Cleopatra, Miranda?); whose "I" has been erased in the act of writing himself down. Each "I" in "Shakespeare" is triply significant, since it refers to the character him- or herself, the actor who plays that character, and the author who wrote the words that actor/character speaks. "Shakespeare" plays with the possibility inherent in the multiple constructions by which "I" can be understood: "I am not what I am," as Iago once again says; so too Othello when he says at that climactic moment of the play, seeming finally to have given up everything of the identity signified by his name, and, in so doing, to have become that empty and hollow nothing that Joel Fineman calls "the sound of *O* in *Othello*":[15] "That's he that was Othello. Here I am" (5.2.284).

The separation that divides "Othello" from his "I" may be understood to construct the space between the person "Shakespeare"—

that historical subject—and the plays he wrote, his literary body. "The play's the thing" that will continue to explore how subjectivity can be read and performed, how the inwardness of their author cannot ever be deciphered, how the appearance of the author in the text is always deceptive, is never exactly the index to his soul, how what seems to be said encodes what is not said. "Shakespeare" will always be an absent presence, spoken but not seen, suggested but physically missing (literally offstage), erased from the text as Hamlet is erased when he says, "The rest is silence" (5.2.341); as Isabella who does not speak in response to the Duke's command "Give me your hand and say you will be mine" (5.1.490) is erased; as Desdemona, strangled in her bed until she cannot speak, is erased; as Cordelia who begins by speaking "Nothing" (1.1.86) and ends being carried out in her father's arms, now truly mute, is erased; as Prospero who drowns his book is erased.

I will close by returning to Foucault, who describes a reading that no longer asks,

Who really spoke? Is it really he and not someone else? With what authenticity or originality? And what part of his deepest self did he express in his discourse? Instead there would be other questions, like these: What are the modes of existence of this discourse? Where has it been used, how can it circulate, and who can appropriate it for himself? What are the places in it where there is room for possible subjects? Who can assume these various subject functions? And behind all these questions, we would hear hardly anything but the stirring of an indifference: What difference does it make who is speaking?[16]

No difference if, as Hamlet says, "The play's the thing" that reveals, as a mirror will, not only the soul of an age now four hundred years past but our own selves as well; not only the absence of its author, whose words we still read and hear performed on the stage, but his mysterious presence as well; not only what might have taken place offstage when Hamlet's father slept in his orchard, when Ophelia wandered too close to the stream, when Hamlet bound for England "fingered their packet" but also what we cannot know, language incapable of making physically present the actions that words "represent" (things we "see" in words that imagine them). No difference if we mean to read the text as an index not of its author's face but of itself, as words set loose in the space (body) of the text, where they range around, centered by the gravitational weight and spin and momentum of their neighbors (also words), against which at any moment one of us is likely to collide.

Notes

PREFACE

1. For *Hamlet* as the most celebrated of Shakespeare's plays, see Terence Hawkes's assessment of the current value of its stock in what he calls "English literature": "At one time, this must obviously have been an interesting play written by a promising Elizabethan playwright. However, equally obviously, that is no longer the case. Over the years, *Hamlet* has taken on a huge and complex symbolizing function and, as a part of the institution called 'English literature,' it has become far more than a mere play by a mere playwright. Issuing from one of the key components of that institution, not Shakespeare, but the creature 'Shakespeare', it has been transformed into the utterance of an oracle, the lucubration of a sage, the masterpiece of a poet-philosopher replete with transcendent wisdom about the way things are, always have been, and presumably always will be" (*Meaning by Shakespeare* [London and New York: Routledge, 1992], 4). See also Hawkes, "The Old Bill—*Hamlet* and the Canon," in Hamlet: *New Critical Essays*, ed. Arthur F. Kinney (New York: Routledge, 2002).

As for Hamlet's many uncertainties, see Stephen Greenblatt's argument that there is "a pervasive pattern, a deliberate forcing together of radically incompatible accounts of almost everything that matters in *Hamlet*. Is Hamlet mad or only feigning madness? Does he delay in the pursuit of revenge or only berate himself for delaying? Is Gertrude innocent or was she complicit in the murder of her husband? Is the strange account of the old king's murder accurate or distorted? Does the Ghost come from Purgatory or from Hell?—for many generations now audiences and readers have risen to the challenge and found that each of the questions may be powerfully and convincingly answered on both sides. What is at stake is more than a multiplicity of answers. The opposing positions challenge each other, clashing and sending shock waves through the play" (*Hamlet in Purgatory* [Princeton: Princeton University Press, 2001], 240). For Hamlet's delay in particular, see Margreta de Grazia's interpretation of the history of *Hamlet* criticism from 1800 to 2000 (particularly focusing on Hegel, Bradley, Freud, Lacan, and Derrida) as a criticism whose "task . . . has been to discover the cause of Hamlet's delay, the cause that prevents him from advancing toward his designated end" ("Teleology, Delay, and the 'Old Mole'," *Shakespeare Quarterly* 50 [1999], 251–67).

There have been a number of other remarkable studies of *Hamlet* published during the last thirty years, including David Leverenz, "The Woman in Hamlet: An Interpersonal View" and Joel Fineman, "Fratricide and Cuckoldry: Shakespeare's Doubles," both in *Representing Shakespeare: New Psychoanalytic Essays*, ed. Murray M. Schwartz and Coppélia Kahn (Baltimore: Johns Hopkins University Press, 1980); Jacques Lacan, "Desire and the Interpretation of Desire in *Hamlet*," in *Literature and Psychoanalysis: The Question of Reading: Otherwise*, ed. Shoshana Felman (Baltimore: Johns Hopkins University Press, 1982); Margaret W. Ferguson, "*Hamlet*: letters and spirits," Terence Hawkes, "Telmah," and Elaine Showalter, "Representing Ophelia: Women, Madness, and the Responsibilities of Feminist Criticism," all in *Shakespeare and the Question of Theory*, ed. Patricia Parker and Geoffrey Hartman (New York and London: Methuen, 1985); Jacqueline Rose, "Sexuality in the Reading of Shakespeare: *Hamlet* and *Measure for Measure*," in *Alternative Shakespeares*, ed. John Drakakis (London and New York: Routledge, 1985), rev. and repr. as "Hamlet—the *Mona Lisa* of Literature" in *Shakespeare and Gender: A History*, ed. Deborah E. Barker and Ivo Camps (London and New York: Verso, 1995); C. L. Barber and Richard P. Wheeler, "Sight Lines on *Hamlet* and Shakespearean Tragedy," in *The Whole Journey: Shakespeare's Powers of Development* (Berkeley: University of California Press, 1986); Stanley Cavell, "Hamlet's Burden of Proof," in *Disowning Knowledge in Six Plays of Shakespeare*

(Cambridge: Cambridge University Press, 1987); Marjorie Garber, "*Hamlet*: Giving Up the Ghost," in *Shakespeare's Ghost Writers* (London and New York: Methuen, 1987); Karin S. Coddon, "'Suche Strange Desygns': Madness, Subjectivity, and Treason in *Hamlet* and Elizabethan Culture," in *Renaissance Drama: New Series 1989* 20 (1989); Janet Adelman, "Man and Wife Is One Flesh: *Hamlet* and the Confrontation with the Maternal Body," in *Suffocating Mothers: Fantasies of Maternal Origin in Shakespeare's Plays, "Hamlet" to "The Tempest"* (London and New York: Routledge, 1992); Valerie Traub, "Jewels, Statues and Corpses: Containment of Female Erotic Power," in *Desire and Anxiety: Circulations of Sexuality in Shakespearean Drama* (London and New York: Routledge, 1992), rev. and repr. in *Shakespeare and Gender*; Patricia Parker, "*Othello* and *Hamlet*: Dilation, Spying, and the 'Secret Place' of Woman," in *Shakespeare Reread: The Text in New Contexts*, ed. Russ McDonald (Ithaca, NY: Cornell University Press, 1994), rev. and repr. as "*Othello* and *Hamlet*: Spying, Discovery, Secret Faults," in *Shakespeare from the Margins: Language, Culture, Context* (Chicago: University of Chicago Press, 1996); Lisa Jardine, "Afterword: What Happens in *Hamlet*," in *Shakespeare and Gender*; Patricia Parker, "'Conveyers Are You All': Translating, Conveying, Representing, and Seconding in the Histories and *Hamlet*," in *Shakespeare from the Margins*; Philip Armstrong, "Watching *Hamlet* watching: Lacan, Shakespeare and the mirror/stage," in *Alternative Shakespeares*, vol. 2, ed. Terence Hawkes (London and New York: Routledge, 1996); Philippa Berry, "Echoic Language and Tragic Identity: *Hamlet*," in *Shakespeare's Feminine Endings* (London and New York: Routledge, 1999); Arthur F. Kinney, ed., Hamlet: *New Critical Essays* (New York: Routledge, 2002); Graham Holdeness, "Visions and Revisions: *Hamlet*," in *Textual Shakespeare: Writing and the Word* (Hatfield, England: University of Hertfordshire Press, 2003); and Stephen Greenblatt, "Speaking with the Dead," in *Will in the World* (New York: W. W. Norton, 2004). My understanding of the play is informed by and indebted to these works.

2. All references to Shakespeare's plays are to *The Complete Pelican Shakespeare*, ed. Stephen Orgel and A. R. Braunmuller (New York: Penguin Putnam Inc., 2002).

3. *Imaginary Audition: Shakespeare on Stage and Page* (Berkeley: University of California Press, 1989), xii. Berger, Jr.'s brilliant account of the argument between performance-centered (or New Histrionicist)

and text-centered reading proposes an approach that "involves an attempt to reconstruct text-centered reading in a way that incorporates the perspective of imaginary audition and playgoing; an attempt to put into play an approach that remains text-centered but focuses on the interlocutory politics and theatrical features of performed drama so as to make them impinge at every point on the most suspicious and antitheatrical of readings" (xiv). See also Berger, Jr.'s earlier thinking on the same subject in "Text Against Performance in Shakespeare: The Example of *Macbeth*," in *The Power of Forms in the English Renaissance*, ed. Stephen Greenblatt (Norman, OK: Pilgrim Books, 1982), 49–81, repr. in *Making Trifles of Terrors* (Stanford: Stanford University Press, 1997), 98–112. For other notable contributions to performance-centered criticism, see for example James C. Bulman, ed., *Shakespeare, Theory, and Performance* (London: Routledge, 1996); Kent Cartwright, *Shakespearean Tragedy and Its Double: The Rhythms of Audience Response* (University Park: Pennsylvania State University Press, 1991); Richard David, *Shakespeare in the Theatre* (Cambridge: Cambridge University Press, 1978); Richard Levin, *New Readings vs. Old Plays: Recent Trends in the Reinterpretation of English Renaissance Drama* (Chicago: University of Chicago Press, 1979), and "Performance-Critics *vs* Close Readers in the Study of English Renaissance Drama," *Modern Language Review* 81 (1986), 545–59; Robert Shaughnessy, ed., *Shakespeare in Performance* (London and New York: Macmillan and St. Martin's Press, 2000); J. L. Styan, *The Shakespeare Revolution* (1977; repr. Cambridge: Cambridge University Press, 1983); Gary Taylor, *Moment by Moment by Shakespeare* (London: Macmillan, 1985); Marvin and Ruth Thompson, ed., *Shakespeare and the Sense of Performance: Essays in the Tradition of Performance Criticism in Honor of Bernard Beckerman* (London and Toronto: Associated University Presses, 1989); William B. Worthen, "Deeper Meanings and Theatrical Technique: The Rhetoric of Performance Criticism," *Shakespeare Quarterly* 40:4 (1989), 441–55; repr. in *Shakespeare : An Anthology of Criticism and Theory 1945–2000*, ed. Russ McDonald (Oxford and Malden, MA: Blackwell, 2004), 762–76.

4. Patricia Parker, *Shakespeare from the Margins*, 273n3. Parker's analysis of "the language of particular plays and its embedding in various contexts in the early modern period starts . . . from its historical dimensions, including interconnections difficult to recognize without an awareness of resonances lost on modern ears" (1). See also Russ Mc-

Donald's claim that "recent critical thought has created new possibilities for reading. Modifications in our understanding of the Shakespearean text, an augmented field of collateral texts available for reading, a subtler sense of the author and textual authority, the return of rhetorical study in a new and more sophisticated guise, the increased importance of politics in virtually all discussion of literature, the prominence of newly considered topics such as race and gender—all these shifts in the critical atmosphere make it necessary to reconsider how the close reading of Shakespeare ought to be done and what results it might produce" ("Introduction," in *Shakespeare Reread*, 10). For a decidedly different view of close reading, one that only appears to be ahistorical and apolitical, see Stephen Booth's essay (included in the same volume) "Close Reading without Readings," which argues for "reading that tries to avoid resulting in 'readings'—in interpretations"; reading that admits "that locally unharnessed, locally unharnessable senses for words and phrases can function in the sentences that contain them—can function valuably without being delivered (or even noticed by anyone but the critic who points them out)"; reading that tries to "think about casual, unobtrusive, substantively irrelevant relationships among *meanings* . . . and to think about such relationships in a way analogous to the way one might think about the relationship among notes of music that present a melody and those that do not"; and reading that notices "substantively irrelevant, ordinarily unobserved affinities among words in sentences and speeches in which the meanings that bond them may be inactive" (43–45). As Booth explains it, the difference between his goals in close reading and those of other critics, "who purposefully come between what is read and readers who think they comprehend it and tell those readers what a text 'really' means," is that, "[u]nlike most close readers, I do not suggest that, say, a meaning for a word that a context invites, but that syntax does not, should or could—once I've advertised it—be included in a paraphrase of the sentence in which it appears" (43).

5. "Performance asks us to submit to its spell, and the text asks us to examine the implications of that submission" (*Making Trifles of Terrors*, 103). Berger, Jr.'s essay sets out to distinguish between "spectators and readers" (who, according to René Girard, "cannot fail to be affected, and cannot refrain from experiencing Shylock's defeat as if it were their own victory" ["'To entrap the wisest': A Reading of *The Merchant of Venice*," in *Literature and Society*, Selected Papers from the English Institute, n.s. 3

(1978), ed. Edward W. Said (Baltimore: Johns Hopkins University Press, 1980), 117]), and goes on to argue "not only that the text differs from the script but also that the Shakespeare play, as a text to be interpreted by readers, provides a critique of the play as a script—that is as the basis of performance" (99). Among the many instances of Berger, Jr.'s thinking about the difference between text and performance, reading and playgoing, note the following: "Because the text as a unit mediates between us and absent speakers it denominates, because it is not dismembered to be distributed among the several bodily loci of speaking performers, we are free to interfere with the speaker/speech assignment, free to explore the 'umbrella' potentiality of words by uncoupling them, abstracting them, and holding them over the play or transferring them to another speaker. . . . The ideological consequences of the distinction between text and performance may be derived from the following two factors. First, theatrical distribution correlates with the irreversible temporality of performance, one speech following another in a syntagmatic flow the predictability of which is guaranteed, *pre-scribed*, by the script; textual deceleration and dislocation, on the other hand, interrupt temporality and gather utterances together into countertemporal or paradigmatic groupings. Second, theatrical distribution accentuates the positional status of the embodied speakers as individuals who produce and 'own' their speeches, while dislocation challenges both the private ownership of speeches and the individualism of speakers" (102–3).

6. *Shakespeare After Theory* (New York and London: Routledge, 1999), 40. Kastan's phrase occurs in the following passage, which argues for an approach to Shakespeare that moves "us from a critical practice that would look *through* the surface of the text in search of the authentic—and authorial—meanings supposedly lurking somewhere (where?) below to one that aggressively looks *at* the text, where meanings are in fact collaboratively made and engaged, constructed and contested. This is not, I would insist, to evade the necessity of reading by replacing a fantasy of authorial presence with a new one of self-evident materiality; it is only to clarify what it is that is read" (40). Like Kastan's "meanings," which he finds by looking *at* rather than *through* a text, the "meanings" of offstage action that I find in *Hamlet* are also "collaboratively made and engaged, constructed and contested" by readers or playgoers who discover them, in their experiences of the play—which are unpredictable and ever-changing, multiple and democratic, culturally based and historically

dependent—and in so doing make them possible. Recognizing its clearly valuable contributions to our understanding of the historicity of Shakespeare's texts, the blindspot of Kastan's "after theory" project, which proposes that "historical scholarship can at least partially recover and restore to view" (32) those circumstances in which Shakespeare's texts were originally written and produced (and which he admits he sometimes, "usually gleefully," has come to think of as "The New Boredom," probably because it delights in what Adorno, criticizing Benjamin, called the "wide-eyed presentation of mere facts" [18]), is that it has so little time actually to read the words that "The AVTHOR/Mr. William Shakespeare" (as Ben Jonson's poem in the Folio identifies him) wrote. My project here—which will take all the time *I* have—addresses that oversight by returning from the historicity of Shakespeare's original production of words to what was produced (those words), "reproduced" now in a number of edited versions, none of them authentically Shakespeare's text but as close as we can get—notwithstanding the possibility of an original manuscript, reproductions of which would still not make Shakespeare contemporaneous, nor any less historic than he now is.

7. Suggesting that a play's words can only be fully "realized" when read on the page, I have stepped into troubled waters. Performance-centered criticism claims just the opposite, that the words of Shakespeare's plays will be "realized" only when they are performed by actors onstage. William B. Worthen notes for example the following: "Shakespeare's plays were written for the theatre, and only in the theatre develop their full impact" (Richard David, *Shakespeare in the Theatre* [Cambridge: Cambridge University Press, 1978], 1); "Shakespeare's words, deliberately designed by a theatrical genius for a thrust stage with live actors and an immediately responding audience, cannot be satisfactorily explored or experienced in any medium but his own" (Homer Swander, "In Our Time: Such Audiences We Wish Him," *Shakespeare Quarterly* 35 [1984]: 540); and "Readers and critics have become increasingly aware that the plays were written for performance and reveal their true natures only in performance" (John Russell Brown, *Discovering Shakespeare: A New Guide to the Plays* [New York: Columbia University Press, 1981], 1) ("Deeper Meanings and Theatrical Technique: The Rhetoric of Performance Criticism," in *Shakespeare: An Anthology of Criticism and Theory 1945–2000*, ed. Russ McDonald [Oxford and Malden, MA: Blackwell, 2004], 766). The claims of such critics derive from the fact that Shake-

speare's plays were written as scripts to be performed rather than texts to be read. Stephen Orgel considers these ideas in a number of different essays: "One indisputable fact about the plays is that they were written not for publication but for performance: they are, in their inception at least, not books but scripts, designed to be realized on the stage" ("The Authentic Shakespeare," *Representations* 21 [1988]; repr. in *The Authentic Shakespeare* [New York and London: Routledge, 2002], 237); "In 'What Is a Text?' I argued for the radical instability of Renaissance dramatic texts, and ended by observing that the dramatic text in its own time was not the play: the text was a script, and it was only where the play started; the play, and its evolution into the texts that have come down to us, was a collaboration between author and actors, with the author by no means the controlling figure in the collaboration" ("What Is a Character?" *Text* 8 [1996]; repr. in *The Authentic Shakespeare*, 7); "the idea of a book embodying the final, perfected state of a literary work was not a Renaissance one, and what the Renaissance practice produced was an edition in which it was unlikely that any copy of a book would be identical to any other copy. . . . The text in flux, the text as process, was precisely what Renaissance printing practice—whether for economic or philosophical reasons—preserved" ("What Is an Editor?" *Shakespeare Studies* 24 [1996]; repr. in *The Authentic Shakespeare*, 15). See also Kastan, who notes that Shakespeare's "plays were not autonomous and self-contained literary objects but provisional scripts for performance, inevitably subjected to the multiple collaborations of production both in the playhouse and in the printing house, where, of course, actors, prompters, collaborators, annotators, revisers, copyists, compositors, printers, and proofreaders all would have a hand in shaping the play-text" (33); and "Shakespeare's cultural preeminence usually obscures for us the fact that he too wrote in such circumstances [i.e., for a theater that "frustrates literary aspirations, dispersing authority for the play among various agents—collaborators and revisers, bookkeepers and prompters, musicians and carpenters, and, of course, the actors themselves—all of whom bear some responsibility for the play's eventual shape and success"] that his artistry was indeed imbedded in commercial, institutional, and material conditions that subordinated his literary talent to practical and pragmatic theatrical concerns" (73).

8. Kastan, 33, 32, 42.

9. Email correspondence with Harry Berger, Jr.,, August 15, 2003.

Berger, Jr. explores the idea of reading the fictions of representation and performance in portrait painting in *The Fictions of the Pose: Rembrandt Against the Italian Renaissance* (Stanford: Stanford University Press, 2000).

10. Statement for Alain Jacquet's U.S. Exhibition, Alexander Iolas Gallery, New York, 1964; quoted in Hardy Blechman, *Disruptive Pattern Material: An Encyclopedia Of Camouflage* (New York: FireFly Books, 2004), 276. Here is Ashbery's statement in context: "The point of camouflaging something is to have it be indistinguishable from the surrounding nature. By comparing camouflage to Cubism, Picasso is saying that the essence of an object may be altogether different in appearance. Cubism . . . is like camouflage which obliterates by pressing a thing as far as possible back into the waves of otherness that surround it."

11. T. J. Clark, *Farewell to an Idea: Episodes from a History of Modernism* (New Haven: Yale University Press, 2001). Here is Clark's statement in context: "If PRESENCE = CONVEXITY, then everything in painting ultimately turns on the artist's success in establishing a strong, cored, convex form in and against an opposite flatness or void. And in practice this basic illusion depends on the engineering a *not*-seen, a *not*-seeable. . . . The moment of maximum visual information in a picture is that at which the object goes out of sight."

12. See for example Stephen Orgel's claim in "What Is a Text?" that the idea of the authentic Renaissance text, particularly a dramatic one, is a fiction of the modern imagination. Citing the work of E. A. J. Honigmann in *The Stability of Shakespeare's Text* (1965) and Gerard Bentley in *The Profession of Dramatist in Shakespeare's Time* (1971), Orgel notes "how much the creation of a play was a collaborative process, with the author by no means at the center of the collaboration. The company commissioned the play, usually stipulated the subject, often provided the plot, often parceled it out, scene by scene, to several playwrights. The text thus produced was a working model, which the company then revised as seemed appropriate. The author had little or no say in these revisions: the text belonged to the company, and the authority represented by the text . . . is that of the company, the owners, not that of the playwright, the author. This means that if it is a performing text we are dealing with, it is a mistake to think that in our editorial work what we are doing is getting back to an author's original manuscript: the very notion of 'the author's original manuscript' is in such cases a fig-

ment. . . . [w]hen we make our editions, of Shakespeare or any other dramatist, we are *not* 'getting back to the author's original text.' We know nothing about Shakespeare's original text" (*Research Opportunities in Renaissance Drama* 24 [1981]; repr. in *The Authentic Shakespeare* (2–3, 5). Greenblatt also considers the problem of the authentic Shakespearean text, noting that "[i]ndeed in the case of Shakespeare (and of the drama more generally) there has probably never been a time since the early eighteenth century when there was less confidence in the 'text.' Not only has a new generation of textual historians undermined the notion that a skilled editorial weaving of folio and quarto readings will give us an authentic record of Shakespeare's original intentions, but theater historians have challenged the whole notion of the text as the central, stable focus of theatrical meaning" (*Shakespearean Negotiations: The Circulation of Social Energy in Renaissance England* [Berkeley: University of California Press, 1988], 3). Kastan's discussion of the problem focuses on the differences between modern edited editions of the plays: "Shakespeare's *King Lear* and Shakespeare's *Hamlet*, as their covers proclaim, turn out to be something less than truth in advertising. They are more properly Alfred Harbage's *King Lear* or Kenneth Muir's, Harold Jenkins's *Hamlet* or Maynard Mack's, the editorial work of selecting and consolidating material from the variant evidence of the early textual witnesses producing a text that, ironically, in its very commitment to Shakespeare's authority (a commitment to 'the principle,' as the Victorian editor Charles Knight said, 'that not a line which appears to have been written by Shakespeare ought to be lost') is different from any that Shakespeare ever intended, as well as different, by virtue of its individual editorial decisions, from any other edited version" (61).

CHAPTER I

1. Terrence Hawkes's description of Barnardo's and Francisco's stage entrance preceding the play's opening words ("Who's there?") suggests the offstage action that we in the audience are asked to imagine has preceded the play: "It begins without words. A man walks out onto the stage and takes up his position, evidently as a sentry. Another man, also evidently a sentry, follows shortly after him. Approaching the first man, the second suddenly halts, seems apprehensive and afraid. The long military spear he is carrying, the partisan, is quickly brought into an offensive position. That movement—before a word is spoken—immediately

pushes the action forward: it enters a different dimension. A mystery has been posited (why are the sentries nervous, why do they make elementary mistakes of military discipline?) and a story starts to unfold" ("Telmah," in *Shakespeare and the Question of Theory*, ed. Patricia Parker and Geoffrey Hartman [New York and London: Methuen, 1985], 310).

2. As Patricia Parker points out, "the play ends by promising, beyond its own theatrical spectacle, the narrative of Horatio/*oratio* that is to report Hamlet's story faithfully to those who could not see or ocularly witness it" ("*Othello* and *Hamlet*: Spying, Discovery, Secret Faults," in *Shakespeare from the Margins: Language, Culture, Context* [Chicago: University of Chicago Press, 1996], 257). See also Anthony Brennan, who notes the offstage action that will supposedly take place after the play is finished: "Horatio in *Hamlet*, it can be argued, has to survive the slaughter since he is the only person who could unfold the details to Fortinbras and the amazed court of the carnage that has invaded the stage—and a very long evening it promises to be offstage, which he previews in a concise, general survey anticipating that detailed report" (*Onstage and Offstage Worlds in Shakespeare's Plays* [London and New York: Routledge, 1989], 11).

3. Several critics have discussed the phenomenon of offstage action in Shakespeare, how speeches are used to deliver actions not performed physically. Brennan points out that "[p]lays are not composed simply of characters enmeshed in sequences of action performed in the presence of an audience. They are a complex weave of actions and reactions, of events that we see and events we hear about performed offstage" (3); Francis Berry looks at how "Insets"—Mercutio's Queen Mab speech, Prospero's speech about his arrival on the island, Ophelia's account of Hamlet's visit to her closet, Gertrude's report of Ophelia's death in the stream—function in the play's "union of language *and* spectacle . . . of something heard or listened to *and* of something seen," and claims that in *Hamlet* they "are corridors retreating to an enigmatic but fascinating hinterland, often minatory or pathetic, and it is this hinterland, which builds up behind the imprisoned *Hamlet* exposed on the stage, that gives this play its depth" (*The Shakespeare Inset: Word and Picture* [New York: Theatre Arts Books, 1965] 1, 143). See also Frances Ann Shirley's *Shakespeare's Use of Off-Stage Sounds* (Lincoln: University of Nebraska Press, 1963). More recently, Celia Daileader's *Eroticism on the Renaissance Stage: Transcendence, Desire, and the Limits of the Visible*

(London and New York: Routledge, 1998) takes up the question of action not performed on the Renaissance stage, i.e., "what we would now call 'heterosexual' erotic activity, despite the obvious complication posed by the absence of female performers," in plays performed in London's commercial theaters between 1595 (*Romeo and Juliet*) and 1621 (*Women Beware Women*). Daileader notes the presence of "erotic activity" in 216 (95.6%) of the 226 plays she examines. Finally, Peter Stallybrass implicitly raises the question of offstage action, what cannot be seen (in this case, what cannot be seen beneath the clothes of the boy actor playing the woman's part), when he focuses on "bed scenes" in plays like *Othello*, specifically on those moments when the play calls for the boy actor to take off his clothes. "What did a Renaissance audience see when boy actors undressed on stage?" he asks, and goes on to argue that "on the Renaissance stage the demand that the spectator *sees* is at its most intense in the undressing of the boy actor, at the very moment when *what* is seen is most vexed, being the point of intersection between spectatorship, the specular, and the speculative" ("Transvestism and the 'body beneath': Speculating on the boy actor," in *Erotic Politics: Desire on the Renaissance Stage*, ed. Susan Zimmerman [London and New York: Routledge, 1992], 64–83).

4. Greenblatt argues that Shakespeare's "crucial breakthrough" in *Hamlet* was the discovery that he "could immeasurably deepen the effect of his plays, that he could provoke in the audience and in himself a peculiarly passionate intensity of response, if he took out a key explanatory element, thereby occluding the rationale, motivation, or ethical principle that accounted for the action that was to unfold. The principle was not the making of a riddle to be solved, but the creation of a strategic opacity. This opacity, Shakespeare found, released an enormous energy that had been at least partially blocked or contained by familiar reassuring explanations" (*Will in the World* [New York: W. W. Norton, 2004], 323–24). Though he does not mention him explicitly, Greenblatt's argument works, if only coincidentally, to answer Eliot's famous critique that *Hamlet* "is full of some stuff that the writer could not drag to light, contemplate, or manipulate into art" ("Hamlet," in *Selected Essays, 1917–1932* [New York: Harcourt, Brace, 1932], 124).

5. The context of Parker's remarks suggests that the "evidence" of action not performed onstage is indeed central to *Hamlet*: "Hamlet's fascination with seeing or uncovering the secrets of his mother has been the

focus of much psychoanalytic criticism of the play—indeed, one of the founding texts of psychoanalysis itself. This queen is the woman who betrays her son first as a mother, a woman whose sexuality is something secret or withheld from him, and then in the opacity and ambiguities of her complicity with Claudius, the man who killed his father and lay with his mother, though in which order is unclear. It is this that produces the sense in *Hamlet* that the play turns on the pivot of an offstage primal scene beyond the reach of vision, a scene on which gazing is forbidden, even in the deflected re-presentation of the player's 'show'—the reason, perhaps, why this *dramatic* show includes its bitter double entendres on the 'o' or 'no-thing' that is woman. This desire to open up to 'shew' involves the sense of a fault or crime that, at least as centrally as Claudius's, involves an offstage secret the entire play comes belatedly after and then attempts recursively to bring to light" (261).

6. "'Sentences serve to describe how things are', we think. The sentence as a picture" (Ludwig Wittgenstein, *Zettel* [Berkeley: University of California Press, 1967], 44e). Wittgenstein also distinguishes between pictures and thought, pictures and images, and images and what he calls "heard sound": "'At that moment the thought was before my mind.'— And how?—'I had this picture.'—So was the picture the thought? No; for if I had just told someone the picture, he would not have got the thought" (44e); "Images are not pictures. I do not tell what object I am imagining by the resemblance between it and the image. Asked 'What image have you?' one can answer with a picture" (109e); [o]ne would like to say: The imaged is in a different *space* from the heard sound. (Question: Why?) The seen is in a different space from the imaged.

Hearing is connected with listening; forming an image of a sound is not.

That is why the heard sound is in a different space from the imagined sound." (109e)

7. Gertrude Stein, "Plays," in *Writings and Lectures 1909–1945* (Baltimore: Penguin Books, 1971), 65.

8. As Brennan puts it, "Reports can imaginatively transport us from 'here' to 'there,' and because of the power of poetry they can also transport us from 'here' to another 'here,' making by an alchemical process gold out of dross, scenery which never has to be accounted for in a production budget. . . . Shakespeare can make us see what is not to be seen, what is offstage, but he can also show us how a character can make oth-

ers see what has never happened, or can describe what has happened in a way that makes it clear he has seen or sees things in different ways from the audience and other characters" (12). When Edgar tells Gloucester what he sees looking down from the cliffs at Dover, for example, "[t]he description . . . does not apply only to what we can see in physical terms but also to the pictures that it evokes in the mind's eye. We are induced to 'see' the figure gathering samphire from his perilous perch half-way down the cliffs. We see the fishermen far beneath on the beach who seem to be no bigger than mice. We see the surge of surf over the pebbles of the beach, and its murmuring sound is evoked even though we are assured that we are so high up that we cannot hear it. The scene vividly described in 14 lines is so compelling that we may feel, as Edgar claims for himself, a sensation of vertigo. In other words, we see what Gloucester cannot see, we see what is offstage even when it is claimed to be onstage and when it flatly contradicts the evidence of our eyes" (12). On a play's physical setting or location as offstage action, see also Harry Berger, Jr.'s claim that "[m]ost details of dramatic locale and setting were communicated through the words of the characters. We never see cliffs and heaths, ships and islands, Egypt and Rome. We only hear about them. They belong, we say, to 'the world of the play,' that is, the fictive world that preexists and surrounds its characters, or at least coexists with them on the same ontological plane, and whose creator is the author outside the play. This world may be likened to a pie or cake all but one slice of which—the characters on stage—is missing." Berger, Jr. also notes Stephen Orgel's assertion (in *The Illusion of Power: Political Theater in the English Renaissance* [Berkeley: University of California Press, 1975], 5) that "the Elizabethan public theater encouraged . . . emphasis on the power of the speaking presence: 'The building is primarily an auditorium, designed for speeches and gestures; acting in it will be largely a form of oratory. . . . Elizabethan playhouses . . . were theaters not of settings and scenic machines, not of illusions, but of actors'" (*Making Trifles of Terrors*, 105, 103-04, 438n10).

9. As Stephen Orgel points out, "Characters, that is, are not people, they are elements of a linguistic structure, lines in a drama, and more basically, words on a page. . . . It is, of course, very difficult to think of character in this way, to release character from the requirements of psychology, consistency and credibility, especially when those words on a page are being embodied in actors on a stage. But it is arguably a dif-

ficulty that drama itself accepts, indeed, embraces, and even explicitly at critical moments acknowledges" ("What Is a Character?" in *The Authentic Shakespeare* [London and New York: Routledge, 2002], 8).

10. Eliot's claim that *Hamlet* lacks an "objective correlative," the term he uses to explain why the play (which he calls "the 'Mona Lisa' of literature") is "most certainly an artistic failure," may be usefully understood in relation to the play's absence of performed physical action. As Eliot puts it, "the only way of expressing emotion in the form of art is by finding an 'objective correlative'; in other words, a set of objects, a situation, a chain of events which shall be the formula of that *particular* emotion; such that when the external facts, which must terminate in sensory experience, are given, the emotion is immediately evoked. . . . Hamlet (the man) is dominated by an emotion which is inexpressible, because it is in *excess* of the facts as they appear. And the supposed identity of Hamlet with his author is genuine to this point: that Hamlet's bafflement at the absence of objective equivalent to his feelings is a prolongation of the bafflement of his creator in the face of his artistic problem" ("Hamlet," in *Selected Essays 1917–1932* [New York: Harcourt, Brace, 1932], 124–25). See also Jacqueline Rose's feminist reading of *Hamlet* in relation to Eliot's essay in "Hamlet—the *Mona Lisa* of Literature," in *Shakespeare and Gender: A History*, ed. Deborah E. Barker and Ivo Kamps (London and New York: Verso, 1995), 104–19; an earlier version of this essay appeared as "Sexuality in the Reading of Shakespeare: *Hamlet* and *Measure for Measure*," in *Alternative Shakespeares*, ed. John Drakakis (London and New York: Routledge, 1985), 95–118.

11. "If this were played upon a stage now, I could condemn it as an improbable fiction" (3.4.121–22).

12. In his celebrated essay "On the Value of *Hamlet*," Stephen Booth also notes the "improbability" of the play's action. Claiming that "almost everything else in the play has, in its particular kind and scale, an improbability comparable to the improbability of the discrepancy between Hamlet's real and expected behavior to Ophelia," he points out that "[t]he very fact that the *Hamlet* we know is an editor-made text has furnished an illusion of firm ground for leaping conclusions that discrepancies between the probable and actual actions, statements, tone and diction of *Hamlet* are accidents of its transmission. Thus, in much the spirit of editors correcting printer's errors, critics have proposed stage directions by which, for example, Hamlet can overhear the plot to test Polo-

nius' diagnosis of Hamlet's affliction, or by which Hamlet can glimpse Polonius and Claudius actually spying on his interview with Ophelia. Either of these will make sense of Hamlet's improbable raging at Ophelia in III.i ("On the Value of *Hamlet*, in *Reinterpretations of Elizabethan Drama*, ed. Norman Rabkin and Max Bluestone [New York: Columbia University Press, 1969]; repr. in *Shakespeare: An Anthology of Criticism and Theory 1945–2000*, ed. Russ McDonald [Oxford and Malden, MA: Blackwell, 2004], 225).

13. *Aspects of the Novel* (New York: Harcourt, Brace, 1927), 130.

14. Berger, Jr.'s phrase appears in a discussion of text vs. script, in which he argues "not only that the text differs from the script but also that the Shakespeare play, as a text to be interpreted by readers, provides a critique of the play as a script—that is, as the basis of performance. I hasten to add that obviously if such a critique can be demonstrated we should not expect it to be so thoroughly antitheatrical as to advocate a ban on performance. Rather we should expect the text to solicit our collaboration in producing a performance that metatheatrically dramatizes characteristic limits of the medium" (*Making Trifles of Terrors*, 99).

15. Stephen Booth among many others notes that "the challenger is the wrong man, the relieving sentry and not the one on duty," an example of how *Hamlet* repeatedly provokes "[t]he audience's sensation of being unexpectedly and very slightly out of step." Proposing "to look at *Hamlet* for what it undeniably is, a succession of actions upon the understanding of an audience," Booth argues that "[t]he action that the first scene of *Hamlet* takes upon the understanding of its audience is like the action of the whole, and most of the individual actions that make up the whole. The first scene is insistently incoherent and just as insistently coherent. It frustrates and fulfills expectations simultaneously" ("On the Value of *Hamlet*," 226). See also Terrence Hawkes on the play's opening moments: "At the beginning, it is immediately noticeable that the military are not in complete control: they get things, fundamental things, wrong. Barnardo's challenge (and the play's first line) "Who's there?" is uttered, as Francisco immediately points out, correcting him, by the wrong sentry." Hawkes points out "similar misconceptions" at the end of the play: "Again, it is Horatio who gets it wrong. We know, from what we have seen, that the story which he proposes to recount to the 'yet unknowing world' . . . is not really the way it was. It was not as simple, as like an 'ordinary' revenge play, as that. His solemnity—'All

this can I/Truly deliver'—mocks at the subtleties, the innuendoes, the contradictions, the imperfectly realized motives and sources for action that have been exhibited to us" (310–11).

16. Editors routinely note that "me" is emphatic; Horace Howard Furness points out that "Francisco, as the sentinel on guard, has the right of insisting on the watch-word, which is given in Barnardo's answer" (*A New Variorum Edition of Shakespeare: Hamlet*, ed. Horace Howard Furness [New York: J. B. Lippincott, 1877; repr. New York: Dover Publications, 1963], 4); Harold Jenkins in the Arden edition (London: Methuen, 1982) writes that "[i]t is the sentry on guard who has the right to challenge." In Q1, Francisco is called simply "1st Sentinel," Barnardo "2nd Sentinel."

17. See Jenkins's note: "Whether or not this is the formal password, as often supposed [Malone was the first to propose it, according to Variorum], Barnardo identifies himself as the one on lawful business. Cf. Marcellus at l. 16. But the speech 'is dramatically ironical in view of all that follows' (Dover Wilson)."

18. The word "bed" appears twelve times in *Hamlet* (in only three plays by Shakespeare does it appear more frequently: *Romeo and Juliet* [20], *Othello* [18], and *Cymbeline* [15]), seven of those instances in various references to Gertrude's bed. The Ghost imagines for Hamlet and his audience a pornographic-like picture of offstage action in which "lust, though to a radiant angel linked, /Will sate itself in a celestial bed" (1.5.55–56), and later commands Hamlet to put a stop to the rampant sexual acts he imagines are now taking place there: "Let not the royal bed of Denmark be/A couch for luxury" (1.5.82–83). The Player Queen imagines for everyone watching *The Mousetrap* (including us) how her offstage action in bed will continue to betray her dead former husband: "A second time I kill my husband dead/When second husband kisses me in bed" (3.2.180–81). And as if having absorbed these sexual images, planted first in his mind by his father and then this Player Queen, Hamlet himself first imagines his uncle "in th' incestuous pleasure of his bed" (3.3.90), then pleads with his mother in her bedroom (the scene in which we actually *see* the bed we have heard so much about) not "to live / In the rank sweat of an enseamèd bed" (3.4.91–92), "go . . . to my uncle's bed" (3.4.159), or "Let the bloat king tempt you again to bed" (3.4.182).

19. Strachey's comment on this line suggests how Francisco's being "sick at heart" sounds a tone that will be echoed throughout the play:

"The key-note of the tragedy is struck in the simple preludings of this common sentry's midnight guard, to sound afterwards in ever-spreading vibrations through the complicated though harmonious strains of Hamlet's own watch through a darker and colder night than the senses can feel" (Variorum, 4). Similarly, Arden notes John Dover Wilson's claim that Francisco's line "foreshadows Hamlet."

20. Coleridge's note on the unseen/unheard mouse of this line claims that its "attention to minute sounds,—naturally associated with the recollection of minute objects . . . gives a philosophic pertinency to this image; but it has likewise its dramatic use and purpose. For its commonness in ordinary conversation tends to produce the sense of reality, and at once hides the poet, and yet approximates the reader or spectator to that state in which the highest poetry will appear and in its component parts, though not in the whole composition, really is the language of nature. If I should not speak it, I feel I should be thinking it;—the voice only is the poet's,—the words are my own" (Variorum, 4–5).

21. Frances Ann Shirley, who does not mention the offstage sound of voices or movement that Francisco thinks he hears, notes that "The sounds in *Hamlet* are amazingly varied. In the first act alone there are flourishes, a cock-crow, the roar of cannon, the sepulchral cries of the ghost under the stage, and perhaps a striking clock" (*Shakespeare's Use of Off-Stage Sounds* [Lincoln: University of Nebraska Press, 1961], 142). Coleridge notes "the gradual transition from the silence and the still recent habit of listening in Francisco's 'I think I hear them,'—to the more cheerful call out, which a good actor would observe, in the 'Stand ho! Who s there?'" (Variorium, 5). See also Francis Berry's comments on the relation between what the stage audience and the theater audience hears and sees: "As with other Insets, a stage-audience sees and hears through them, but both the audience *in Hamlet* and the audience *of Hamlet* are in a different order or relation to the show put on for them (*The Shakespeare Inset: Word and Picture* [New York: Theatre Arts Books, 1965], 137).

22. Stephen Greenblatt notes a resonance in Horatio's line ("A piece of him") with both Ophelia being "divided from herself" (4.5.82) and Hamlet being "from himself . . . ta'en away" (5.2.212) (*Hamlet in Purgatory* [Princeton: Princeton University Press, 2001], 211).

23. Coleridge's note on this line suggests the different offstage lives of Horatio and Marcellus, whose relations to Barnardo in his offstage life are also different: "The actor should be careful to distinguish the

expectation and gladness of Barnardo's 'Welcome, Horatio!' from the mere courtesy of his 'Welcome, good Marcellus!'" (Variorum, 6).

24. Terrence Hawkes points to this line as an example of how "looking backwards, re-vision, or reinterpretation, the running of events over again, out of their time sequence, ranks, in fact, as a fundamental mode of *Hamlet*. *Subsequence, posteriority*, these are the effective modes of the opening, generating phrases like 'has *this thing* appear'd *again* tonight'" (313).

25. Terrence Hawkes, *Meaning By Shakespeare* (London and New York: Routledge, 1992), 4. As Hawkes points out, *Hamlet* has become the greatest work of the greatest writer in "English Literature": "it enters our way of life as one of the resources through which that way of life generates meaning. As an aspect of the works of 'Shakespeare,' the play helps to shape large categories of thought, particularly those which inform political and moral stances, modes and types of relationship, our ideas of how men and women, fathers and mothers, husbands and wives, uncles and nephews, sons and daughters ought respectively to behave and interact. It becomes part of a means of first formulating and then validating important power relationships, say between politicians and intellectuals, soldiers and students, the world of action and that of contemplation. Perhaps its probing of the relation between art and social life, role-playing onstage and role-playing in society, appears so powerfully to offer an adequate account of important aspects of our own experience that it ends by constructing them. In other words, *Hamlet* crucially helps to determine how we perceive and respond to the world in which we live. You can even name a cigar after it" (4).

For *Hamlet*'s position at the center of mainstream popular culture, one need only look, as Lynda Boose and Richard Burt do, at its recent film history: "The *Hamlet* created by the 1990s wasn't big just among the literati—he was so big that he was making guest appearances in all sorts of unexpected places. . . . In 1991, Oliver Stone cast the Kennedy assassination through the lens of *Hamlet* in *JFK*. In 1994, Danny DeVito and the US Army found *Hamlet* to be the perfect force for transforming wimps and misfit soldiers into the STRAK army company that concludes *Renaissance Man* . . . reaffirming the male bond in "Sound Off" lyrics that inventively substitute "Hamlet's mother, she's the Queen" for the usual female object of cadenced derision. Similarly, Disney's 1994 *The Lion King* . . . reworked *Hamlet* for a younger generation. In 1995,

Kenneth Branagh released his *A Midwinter's Tale*, a film about a provincial English production of *Hamlet*, and then in 1996 and 1997 his own full-length and abridged versions of *Hamlet* ("Totally Clueless? Shakespeare goes Hollywood in the 1990s," in *Shakespeare, The Movie* [London and New York: Routledge, 1997], 9).

CHAPTER 2

1. "Hamlet returns from his voyage a changed man, with an air of self-possession greater than at any other time of the play. We are not told why; but we may fancy, if we like, that the seas have helped to expel the 'something-settled matter in his heart,' or that he has gained confidence from the hoisting of Rosencrantz and Guildenstern with their own petar, or that simply his 'cause of distemper' is wearing off. The real source of the change is, of course, a technical one. The requirements of tragic drama compel his creator to win back our respect for him before the end, to dissipate the clouds at sunset. Hamlet, we feel, is himself, or almost himself; and we begin to hope once again, though because he is the hero of a tragedy we know that our hope is vain" (*What Happens in Hamlet* [London and New York: Cambridge University Press, 1962], 266–67). Not surprisingly, Wilson's view (first proposed in 1935) echoes that of A. C. Bradley, first stated in 1904: "In what spirit does [Hamlet] return? Unquestionably, I think, we can observe a certain change, though it is not great. First, we notice here and there what seems to be a consciousness of power, due probably to his success in counter-mining Claudius and blowing the courtiers to the moon, and to his vigorous action in the sea-fight. . . . Secondly, we nowhere find any direct expression of that weariness of life and that longing for death which were so marked in the first soliloquy and in the speech 'To be or not to be.' This may be a mere accident, and it must be remembered that in the Fifth Act we have no soliloquy. . . . And, in the third place, there is a trait about which doubt is impossible,—a sense in Hamlet that he is in the hands of Providence" (*Shakespearean Tragedy* [New York: St. Martins, 1957], 114–15) For similar views, see Harold C. Goddard, who quotes Wilson in claiming that "There are those who describe his indubitably changed attitude as a new 'air of self-possession.' It would be nearer the mark to call it the calmness of desperation, though it is far from being all calmness" (*The Meaning of Shakespeare*, vol. 1 [Chicago: University of Chicago Press, 1951], 373–74); and Maynard Mack, who claims that Hamlet

"has now learned, and accepted, the boundaries in which human action, human judgment, are enclosed. Till his return from the voyage he had been trying to act beyond these, had been encroaching on the role of providence. . . . Now, he has learned that there are limits to the before and after that human reason can comprehend. Rashness, even, is sometimes good. Through rashness he has saved his life from the commission for his death, 'and prais'd be rashness for it.' This happy circumstance and the unexpected arrival of the pirate ship make it plain that the roles of life are not entirely self-assigned" ("The World of *Hamlet*," in *Shakespeare: Modern Essays in Criticism* [New York: Oxford University Press, 1957], 255).

2. Several critics have written about the letters in *Hamlet*, among them Stephen Orgel, who sees them as an example of how drama sometimes makes explicit the fact that its characters are not real people but are actually made out of words: "It may seem self-evident that in drama, the character is the script, though it is a truism that drama nevertheless also takes pains to articulate from time to time: Laertes calls Ophelia 'a document in madness' [4.5.178], Hamlet's fight with the pirates consists of Horatio reading aloud from a letter about it (4.6.12ff.): what actors do, after all, is not perform actions but recite lines, and the character is the lines" ("What Is a Character?" in *The Authentic Shakespeare* [London and New York: Routledge, 2002], 8); and Margaret W. Ferguson, who sees them as an instance of how Hamlet becomes as ruthlessly kinglike as Claudius: "It is no accident that Hamlet kills Rosencrantz and Guildenstern by means of a forged letter. For Claudius's letter ordering the king of England to kill Hamlet, Hamlet substitutes a letter ordering the king to kill Rosencrantz and Guildenstern. He seals that letter with his father's ring, the signet or sign of royal power. . . . Claudius says that he cannot understand Hamlet's letter ('What should this mean?' he asks Laertes [IV.vii.47]); but he recognizes Hamlet's 'character' in the handwriting and proceeds quickly enough to give it a kingly interpretation" ("*Hamlet*: letters and spirits," in *Shakespeare and the Question of Theory*, ed. Patricia Parker and Geoffrey Hartman [New York: Methuen, 1985], 299–300). See also Cyrus Hoy, the editor of the Norton Critical Edition of *Hamlet*, who points out that "[f]ollowing the entrance of the Messenger, the King says in *F*, 'How now? What Newes?' and the Messenger replies, 'Letters my Lord from *Hamlet*.' [Harold] Jenkins comments ([*Studies in Bibliography*], XIII, 36): 'In *Q* the King is not told the letters

come from Hamlet; he is left to find this out as he reads, and his cry "From *Hamlet*" betokens his astonishment on doing so. I think Hamlet would not have approved of the *F* messenger who robs his bomb of the full force of its explosion. Shakespeare's messenger did not even know he carried such a bomb, for the letters had reached him via sailors who were ignorant of their sender. They took him for "th' Embassador that was bound for *England*" (IV.vi.10). *F*, with its too knowledgeable messenger, by seeking to enhance the effect, destroys it" (*Hamlet* [New York: W. W. Norton, 1963], 77n); and Orgel, who notes that "at the end of Hamlet's scene with his mother, the following exchange takes place:

> *Ham.* I must to England, you know that?
> *Queen.*   Alack,
>   I had forgot. 'Tis so concluded on.

And in the second quarto, Hamlet continues,

> There's letters sealed, and my two schoolfellows,
> Whom I will trust as I will adders fanged—
> They bear the mandate. . . . (3.4.202ff.) (11)

But the writing of the letters and the mandate to Rosencrantz and Guildenstern are things that have not happened yet; 'the "commission,"' as the Arden editor Harold Jenkins and innumerable editors before him note, 'was still to be prepared.' Jenkins continues, 'As to how Hamlet knew of it, since the text . . . is silent, speculation is invalid. The "difficulty" passes unnoticed in the theatre. . . . '" (11).

3. Returning from life-after-death on the one hand (King Hamlet dies "while sleeping within [his] orchard," 1.5.59) and life-almost-put-to-death on the other (Hamlet avoids death in England by waking from his sleep not in an orchard but in his cabin), Hamlet and his father travel along parallel lines in the play—lines that suggest the degree to which the son's life echoes that of his father. See Richard Halpern's discussion of Jacques Lacan's "Hamlet, par Lacan" (*Orincar* 24 [1981]): "Lacan's play, like Shakespeare's, is directed by a ghost—the ghost of the Father whose law is inscribed on the son. 'To be sure, [Hamlet] has received the express command of his father, admired above all. . . . We have to do here with a play that opens shortly after the death of a father who was, *so his son Hamlet tells us*, a very admirable king. The ideal king and father'. . . . It is the son upon whom it falls to maintain the father's

ideal status—indeed, to create it, as Lacan's skeptical italics suggest." As Halpern goes on to note, Lacan "introduces his analysis of *Hamlet* in the context of the following specimen dream from *The Interpretation of Dreams*: '*His* [the patient's] *father was alive once more and was talking to him in the usual way, but* (the remarkable thing was that) *he had really died, only he did not know it*'," pointing out that "[u]nlike the dead father in Freud's patient's dream, King Hamlet not only knows that he is dead but knows how he has died"—by poison poured into his ears, a death echoed in Hamlet's death (whose body is pierced by Laertes's poisoned sword) and also Claudius's (into whose mouth rather than ear Hamlet pours poison). *Shakespeare Among the Moderns* [Ithaca and London: Cornell University Press, 1997], 255-56, 59)

4. Hamlet—whose voice (in letters) returns from England before his body does (unlike his father, whose ghost returns physically from his "prison house" three scenes before he actually speaks)—actually writes at least four letters (not counting the forged one rewritten to the King of England), all of which arrive at Elsinore before he himself returns "in person": one to Horatio, written after his exit in 4.4 (either aboard the pirate ship or else back on Danish soil) and delivered (by the Sailor) to Horatio in 4.6, who reads it aloud in that scene; at least three others to Claudius and Gertrude, presumably written at the same time and again delivered by a Messenger who gives them to Claudius ("These to your majesty, this to the queen" [4.7.36]), one of which he reads aloud when he gets it (the other or others as well as the one to Gertrude are never mentioned again).

5. Olivier's film also overlooks (fails to "hear") Hamlet's letters to Claudius, to which the letter to Horatio refers and that appear in the following scene where the messenger gives them to Claudius: "These to your majesty, this to the queen" (4.7.36). Only one of these three letters is read aloud in the play, the one to Claudius that reads (cryptically):

> High and mighty, you shall know I am set naked on your kingdom. Tomorrow shall I beg leave to see your kingly eyes; when I shall (first asking your pardon thereunto) recount the occasion of my sudden return. (4.7.42–46)

The fact that Hamlet's letter to Gertrude never appears in the play except as a stage prop in 4.7—she never mentions it, never appears onstage to read it or even to receive it—invites us to ask whether she ever did receive it, and if so what it said, and if not, why not (did Claudius have something to do with it not being delivered to her?). Conversely, if she did get it and read it, again an offstage action that we do not see or ever hear about, did that letter have something to do with Gertrude's actions in the final scene—her drinking wine from a cup that she either knows or does not know is poisoned? (This seems to be Olivier's point in showing this scene, which takes place without words: Osric bringing in the two letters, one for Claudius and one for Gertrude, who, when she begins to read, turns to her right at the bottom of one of the two stairways and walks slowly up, just as Claudius walks up the stairs to the right, husband and wife moving away from one another as they read their respective letters from her son and his nephew, ascending as the scene fades into the black and white silence at the top of the stairs.) Though Olivier shows it in his film, we do not know any of this of course, because it does not appear in the text of Shakespeare's play. And so, as with so much else in *Hamlet*, we are left to imagine what has happened, invited to speculate about things that cannot be known about *Hamlet*—because they are not shown, cannot be seen, are only heard about in the words the play uses to "perform" them.

6. Berger, Jr.'s phrase "surplus meaning" appears in the following passage, which presents as good an argument for the virtues of "close reading" as any I know: "It is hard for us to believe that playgoers understand all the figurative acrobatics executed by Shakespeare's language as it flies by, and it is equally hard to believe that Elizabethan spectators—whether standing in the pit or seated in the tiers . . . were not in the same plight. Since his most magnificently theatrical passages of verse often seem to us to be the most notoriously misinterpreted ones, we suspect that a trap, an antitheatrical comment, lies behind Shakespeare's arousal of what Geoffrey Hartman has called 'the lust of the ears' (*Saving the Text: Literature/ Derrida/Philosophy* [Baltimore: Johns Hopkins University Press, 1981], 123). The language presents itself as having that within which passes show. It often teases or threatens its auditors by making them feel they are hearing more than they need to hear but less than they want to hear. If at first the auditor, like Desdemona listening to Othello, 'with a greedy ear/Devour[s] up my discourse,' there comes a moment when the continual display of withheld surplus meaning converts curiosity to anxiety: 'what does your speech import?/I understand a fury in your words,/But

not the words.' This is the anxiety of, or for, the text that sends us from stage to book to see if we can get a better sense of what is really going on. The shadow of textuality falls across Shakespeare's heard language whenever its rhetorical panoply seems conspicuously to conceal, and to protect us from, surplus meaning" ("Text Against Performance," in *Making Trifles of Terrors: Redistributing Complicities in Shakespeare* [Stanford: Stanford University Press, 1997], 101).

7. Hamlet's cabin is not the only "room or compartment in a vessel for sleeping or eating in" in Shakespeare's plays: *OED* 5 gives *The Tempest* 1.1.14 as an example ("Keep to your cabins, you do assist the storm"). *OED* also cites *Twelfth Night* 1.5.257 ("Make me a willow cabin at your gate") as an example of "cabin" meaning "a temporary shelter of slight materials."

8. *OED* v.2 cites this line as its first example of "scarf" meaning "to wrap (a garment) *about* or *around* a person in the manner of a scarf." Shakespeare also uses "scarf" as a verb in *Macbeth* 3.2.47–48 (Come, sealing night, / Scarf up the tender eye of pitiful day")—*OED* v.1 cites this line as the first example of this meaning ("To clothe, cover or wrap with or as with a scarf or scarves . . . to blindfold"). According to *OED*, "scarf" as a noun originally suggested a military uniform ("A broad band of silk or other material, worn [chiefly by soldiers or officials] either diagonally across the body from one shoulder to the opposite hip, or round the waist"; *OED* cites *Much Ado About Nothing* 2.1.180–82 as an example: "What fashion will you wear the garland of, . . . under your arm, like a lieutenant's scarf?"), which adds to the sense that Hamlet's clothing—as befits this "changed man," this man of action—has something of a military flourish about it.

9. Shakespeare uses "groped" here in the sense of *OED* v2: "To attempt to find something by feeling about as in the dark, or as a blind person; to feel *for* (or *after*) something with the hand." But he also uses "groping" with sexual overtones in *Measure for Measure* 1.2.88, where Pompey tells Mistress Overdone that Claudio's offense was "Groping for trouts in a familiar river" (the "indecent sense" of *OED* 3b, which does not cite this line as an example but does cite it in 2b, where "grope" can be "Applied to the catching of fish, esp. trout, by feeling for them in the water." (See also Eric Partridge, *Shakespeare's Bawdy* [London and New York: Routledge, 1958], 117, which also cites this line). The sexual suggestion of "groping" exploited by Shakespeare in that context seems

to be implicit in his use of "groped" in this speech as well, which appears to push it further when Hamlet goes on to tell Horatio that he "had [his] desire/Fingered their packet . . . withdrew." Shakespeare uses "desire" with sexual overtones elsewhere in *Hamlet*, when Laertes tells Ophelia to "keep you in the rear of your affection,/Out of the shot and danger of desire" (1.3.33–34); also in *A Midsummer Night's Dream*, where Theseus tells Hippolyta that the too-slowly waning prenuptial moon "lingers [his] desires,/Like to a stepdame or a dowager" (1.1.4–5), and *2 Henry IV*, where Poins says of Falstaff "Is it not strange that desire should so many years outlive performance?" (2.4.255–56). Partridge, who points to these examples, also notes the possible sexual meaning of the verb "fingering" ("To caress intimately [the vulgarism is 'to fingerfuck']; intimate caresses"), citing *Pericles* 1.1.82–83 ("You are a fair viol, and your sense the strings;/Who, fingered to make man his lawful music"), *Cymbeline* 2.3.13–14 ("If you can penetrate her with your fingering, so"), and *The Taming of the Shrew* 3.1.64–65, where "Hortensio, amorous wooer in guise of music-teacher, says to Bianca, 'Madam, before you teach the instrument/To learn the order of my fingering,/I must begin with rudiments of art'" (127). Hamlet's "withdrew," which is clearly meant to say what it says here (he left the room), may also perhaps convey—at least in the sexually charged company of these words—a suggestion of the penis withdrawing after penetration.

10. *Hamlet* is of course full of sexually charged language; see for instance the exchange between Hamlet and Ophelia in *The Mousetrap* scene, which I talk about in Chapter Five in relation to Hamlet's speech to Gertrude in her bedroom ("Not this, by no means, that I bid you do" [3.4.181]) and Ophelia's speech to her father about Hamlet's visit to *her* closet ("My lord, as I was sewing in my closet" [2.1.76]), both of which are echoed here—in Hamlet's vision of Claudius "paddling in your neck with his damned fingers" (185) and Ophelia's account of Hamlet's "doublet all unbraced" (77); other sexually charged language in Gertrude's speech on Ophelia's death in 4.7, which I talk about in Chapter Four, is also echoed here—"dead-men's-fingers" (169) and, at least obliquely, "snatches" (175), meaning words of a song but as the verb "snatch" meaning to steal suggesting how Hamlet "Fingered" Rosencrantz and Guildenstern's "packet," which itself echoes "these pickers and stealers" (3.2.329), as he calls the fingers he swears by when he assures Rosencrantz that he still loves him, as well as the "fingers and thumb" (3.2.352)

that he asks Guildenstern to "Govern these ventages [of the recorder] with" (351–52) in that scene; and the story of Hamlet's father "Sleeping within [his] orchard" (1.5.59), the Ghost recalling to Hamlet how "Upon [his] secure hour thy uncle stole" (61) up to him, in his own way "had [his] desire" when he poured the "juice of cursed hebona" (62) into his ears, its "leperous distillment" (64) penetrating "all [his] smooth body" (73)—all of which I will talk about further in Chapter Three.

11. In *Hamlet*, a play about memory, the word "memory" appears ten times—more than in any other play by Shakespeare. "Remember" appears nine times (eleven in *The Tempest*, ten in *Pericles*).

CHAPTER 3

1. Marjorie Garber notes that the physical presence of the Ghost onstage "is a concretization of a missing presence, the sign of what is there by not being there. ''Tis here?' ''Tis there!' ''Tis gone!' cry the sentries (1.1.142–43)" (*Shakespeare's Ghost Writers: Literature as Uncanny Causality* [New York and London: Methuen, 1987], 129). Several other critics have recently mentioned the Ghost's speech in passing. Quoting the entire speech, Terrence Hawkes claims that it is the "most memorable manifestation" of how "the audience of *Hamlet* might legitimately feel that it is being buttonholed, cajoled, persuaded by participants in the play to look back, to 'revise,' to see things again in particular ways, to 'read' or interpret them along specific lines and to the exclusion of others" ("Telmah," in *Shakespeare and the Question of Theory*, ed. Patricia Parker and Geoffrey Hartman [New York and London: Methuen, 1985], 315). Janet Adelman notes "the subterranean logic by which the effects of Claudius's poison on Old Hamlet's body replicate the effects of venereal disease, covering his smooth body with the lazarlike tetter, the 'vile and loathsome crust' . . . that was one of the diagnostic signs of syphilis" (*Suffocating Mothers: Fantasies of Maternal Origin in Shakespeare's Plays, "Hamlet" to "The Tempest"* [London and New York: Routledge, 1992], 26). David Hillman sees it as one instance of the play's concern with "*corporeal* interiority": "The play opens . . . under the pall of the felt absence of Hamlet's father. And it is his innards, perverted from their normal healthfulness by Claudius's 'leperous distilment,' that we hear about in detail first. . . . The Ghost's account strikingly depicts the dual effect of the poison upon his body: an internal thickening, followed immediately by a hardening of the body's boundaries" ("Visceral Knowledge:

Shakespeare, Skepticism, and the Interior of the Early Modern Body," in *The Body in Parts: Fantasies of Corporeality in Early Modern Europe*, ed. David Hillman and Carla Mazzio [London and New York: Routledge, 1997], 91).

2. Stanley Cavell, "Hamlet's Burden of Proof," in *Disowning Knowledge in Six Plays of Shakespeare* (Cambridge: Cambridge University Press, 1987), 181.

3. Claiming that "the skeptical impulse to access the interior of the body takes center stage in *Hamlet*," Hillman also points out a number of passages that demonstrate what he calls Hamlet's "sense of the importance of corporeal insides" (90, 92): "I have that within which passes show" (1.2.85), "I should ha' fatted all the region kites/With this slave's offal" (2.2.518–19), "You go not till I set you up a glass/Where you may see the inmost part of you" (3.4.19–20), "I'll lug the guts into the neighbor room" (3.4.212), "the worm that hath eat of a king . . . [who] may go a progress through the guts of a beggar" (4.3.26–30). Noting these same lines, Stephen Greenblatt argues that Hamlet's exchange with Claudius "extends beyond the cruel and callous joke about Polonius; the supper where the host does not eat but is eaten is the Supper of the Lord. Protestant polemicists had returned throughout the sixteenth century to the moment of eating God's body; it was for them a way of mocking what they took to be the crude materialism of the Catholic doctrine of transubstantiation" (*Hamlet in Purgatory* [Princeton: Princeton University Press, 2001], 240).

4. Terrence Hawkes points out that "by the middle of the play our attention has been forcefully drawn to the death of no fewer than *five* fathers: King Fortinbras; King Hamlet; Polonius; Achilles; and Gonzago, the Player King. In four of the cases an avenging son presents himself: Fortinbras, Hamlet, Laertes, Pyrrhus. The pattern seems to push Hamlet in his role as revenger into the foreground" (316).

5. In a letter to Wilhelm Fliess (October 15, 1897), Freud notes one of the many likenesses between Hamlet and his father: "And does he not in the end, in the same marvelous way as my hysterical patients do, bring down punishment on himself by suffering the same fate as his father of being poisoned by the same rival?" See Arthur F. Kinney, "Introduction," in *Hamlet: New Critical Essays* (New York and London: Routledge 2002), p. 35. Greenblatt also sees a likeness between Hamlet and his father's ghost, who may also "be said to be present

at the end of the play, . . . that is inside his son. When Hamlet first receives his father's dread command, he repeats it to himself, in his own voice, as if he wants to ventriloquize the Ghost's words by making them his 'word': 'Now to my word:/It is "Adieu, adieu, remember me."/I have sworn't' (1.5.111–13). At the close Hamlet does not speak of his father, but he twice bids farewell to Horatio in a strange phrase: 'I am dead' (5.2.275, 270). The phrase simply picks up on what Laertes has told him—'Hamlet, thou art slain' (5.2.256)—and elsewhere in his final speech Hamlet speaks of himself not as a person who is already dead but as one who is dying: 'O, I die . . . I cannot live . . . He has my dying voice . . . O, O, O, O!' (5.2.294–301). But, in the context of the play as a whole, the reiterated expression 'I am dead' has an odd resonance: these are words that are most appropriately spoken by a ghost. It is as if the spirit of Hamlet's father has not disappeared; it has been incorporated by his son" (228–29). Discussing what he calls "deferred representation; Shakespeare's way of presenting in the closing image of a play something denied our sight from the beginning," Stanley Cavell suggests something of the same link when he writes, "Hamlet performs the murder and substitute murder only after announcing that he is dead, thus demonstrating that to take the Ghost's revenge is to become the Ghost" ("Hamlet's Burden of Proof," in *Disowning Knowledge*, 190).

6. Hawkes also points out that *Hamlet* does not actually end "[w]hen the dialogue stops and when the soldiers carry the bodies off and the music and the explosion of the cannons is heard . . . for there follows applause, and then that complex of revisionary ironies, which we group together under the heading of the 'curtain call'" (312). Compare Greenblatt's comment on the significance of the audience's applause in both *1 Henry IV*, where "We are, after all, in the theater, and our pleasure depends upon the fact that there is no escape, and our applause ratifies the triumph of our confinement" ("Invisible Bullets," in *Shakespearean Negotiations: The Circulation of Social Energy in Renaissance England* [Berkeley: University of California Press, 1988], 47) and *The Tempest*, which "comes to an end . . . and then, astonishingly, continues beyond the confines of its plot with the strange spectacle of a theatrical afterlife. Delicately poised between the imaginary world of the play and the commercial world of the theater, between the princely magician and the impoverished actor, Prospero turns directly to the spectators and pleads

for suffrages. . . . He is not, of course, crying out from Purgatory; he is speaking from the stage. And in place of prayers, we offer the actor's ticket to bliss: applause" (*Hamlet in Purgatory*, 260–61).

7. Exemplifying what Geoffrey Hartman has called Shakespeare's "lust of the ears" (*Saving the Text: Literature/Derrida/Philosophy* [Baltimore: Johns Hopkins University Press, 1981], 123; quoted in Harry Berger, Jr., "Text Against Performance," in *Making Trifles of Terrors: Redistributing Complicities in Shakespeare* [Stanford: Stanford University Press, 1997], 101), the word "ear" occurs 24 times in *Hamlet*, more than in any other play by Shakespeare. The word "speak" occurs 64 times, also more than in any other play; "hear" occurs 28 times, second only to *Coriolanus* in Shakespeare. In every instance in which "hear" appears it is accompanied either with the word "speak" or its ideational equivalent, as for example when Hamlet says to Horatio "For God's love let me hear!" (1.2.195) or Laertes says to Ophelia "do not sleep,/But let me hear from you" (1.3.3–4), where Laertes actually means not that Ophelia will speak out loud to him but that she will write him letters that, when he is far away in France and cannot see her in person, he will be able to read (with his eyes) and from those words get an image of what is happening in her life—a verbal picture not unlike the one Hamlet gets (and we in the audience with him) when the Ghost informs him of the events that transpired when he was, as he says, "Sleeping within my orchard,/My custom always of the afternoon" (1.5.59–60).

8. *OED* quotes *Measure for Measure* 2.2.117–18, "Man, proud man,/Drest in a little briefe authoritie," and *Macbeth* 5.5.23–24, "Out, out, briefe candle,/Life's but a walking Shadow."

9. "Said of times, places, action: In which one is free from fear or anxiety," according to *OED* 1d, which cites this line as example.

10. "Hebona" is the spelling in Q1 and Q2; F reads "hebenon." Variorum conjectures about the derivation and pharmacology of "hebona," linking it to henbane (Latin *eberus* and *hebenus*, of which the most common variety is Latin *hyoscyamus niger*), ebony, hemlock, and deadly nightshade (Latin *Solanum maniacum*) (*A New Variorum Edition of Shakespeare: Hamlet*, ed. Horace Howard Furness [New York: J. B. Lippincott, 1877; repr. New York: Dover Publications, 1963], 102). Jenkins's "Longer Note" in Arden, which adds to that list guaiacum and especially yew, goes on to warn us that "it is probably a mistake to seek to equate *hebenon* with any familiar plant. No doubt Shakespeare drew on what he had

heard or read of well-known poisons, but he surely relied . . . on a suggestion of the fabulous to intensify the horror" (457).

11. Patricia Parker suggests that "claustrophobia," which pervades the world of *Hamlet*, "may be one of the resonances in the name of Claudius" (*Shakespeare from the Margins: Language, Culture, Context* [Chicago: University of Chicago Press, 1996], 257).

12. See for instance Jenkins's summary of historical background in his introduction to the Arden edition, where he recounts the story of Francesco Maria I della Rovere, Duke of Urbino, who died in 1538, allegedly after his barber "had poisoned him by a lotion in his ears" (102). Jenkins also notes that Pliny's *Natural History* (xxv.4) mentions "pouring oil of henbane in the ears" (456).

13. *OED* cites these lines as its example for "posset," "curd," and "eager." Notice the ideational and grammatical and phonetic likeness and difference between "did pour" in line 63 and "doth posset" in line 68.

14. Variorum, 103.

15. Adelman notes that "Skin eruptions of the sort the ghost describes were one of the symptoms of syphilis . . . ; Thersites wishes 'tetter' on the 'masculine whore' Patroclus (*Troilus and Cressida*, 5.1.16, 22). Both the ghost's 'crust' and his odd 'bark'd about' are anticipated in early descriptions of the disease: Francisco Lopez de Villalobos notes the 'very ugly eruption of crusts upon the face and body,' Josef Grunbeck the wrinkled black scabs, 'harder than bark'. . . . The description of the poison as a 'leperous distilment' that courses through the body like 'quicksilver' . . . might also further the association of the poison with syphilis, since quicksilver was a routine treatment for syphilis . . . and leprosy itself was associated with venereal disease; for Shakespearean uses of this association, see Timon's punning 'Make the hoar leprosy ador'd' (*Timon*, 4.3.36) and Antony's wishing leprosy on 'yon ribbaudred nag of Egypt,' *Antony*, 3.10.10" (254–55, note 33).

CHAPTER 4

1. Gertrude Stein, "Plays," in *Writings and Lectures 1909–1945* (Baltimore: Penguin Books, 1971), 65.

2. For an early, quintessentially romantic view of the speech and its subject, see Thomas Campbell's account in *Blackwood's Magazine* (1818): "Perhaps this description by the Queen is poetical rather than dramatic; but its exquisite beauty prevails, and Oph[elia], dying and dead, is still

the same Oph[elia] that first won our love. Perhaps the very forgetfulness of her throughout the remainder of the play, leaves the soul at full liberty to dream of the departed. She has passed away from the earth like a beautiful air,—a delightful dream. There would have been no place for her in the agitation and tempest of the final catastrophe. We are satisfied that she is in her grave. And in place of beholding her involved in the shocking troubles of the closing scene, we remember that her heart lies at rest, and the remembrance is like the returning voice of melancholy music." Campbell is still at it in 1833, taking aim this time at Gertrude: "The Queen was affected after a fashion by the picturesque mode of Ophelia's death, and takes more pleasure in describing it than any one would who really had a heart. Gertrude was a gossip,—and she is gross even in her grief" (*A New Variorum Edition of Shakespeare: Hamlet*, ed. Horace Howard Furness [New York: J. B. Lippincott, 1877; repr. New York: Dover Publications, 1963], 370, 73). Granville-Barker notes that Gertrude's speech "gives actuality to Ophelia's unseen death. . . . [It] matches in vividness our last sight of her living. And the beauty and pity of it incidentally help to rescue Gertrude in our eyes from the degradation of Hamlet's painting of her

> In the rank sweat of an enseamed bed,
> Stewed in corruption, honeying and making love
> Over the nasty sty . . .

with the much more to that purpose in the closet scene. She is to have no further very prominent part in the play. We shall remember her as well as Ophelia by this" (*Preface to Hamlet* [New York: Hill and Wang, 1957], 144). Asking "How did the clumsy and wit-disordered girl, all got up with flowers, come to be clambering on the weak branch of a willow that hung 'aslant a Brooke'?" Francis Berry notes "a remarkable discordance between the actual picture the spectators see and the words which the audience hear, words which create for them an imaginative picture utterly different from the actual picture of a castle interior. Abstracting the stage-audience from their *present*, their is-ness, abstracting them from friendly quarrel or querulous friendship (Claudius and Laertes draw together only because they have both been wronged by Hamlet), by translating them to another, though recent, time and to another, though presumably nearby, place, the Queen thereby—and simultaneously—abstracts the theatre-audience from their involvement in the critical moment of the *here*" (*The Shakespeare Inset: Word and Picture* [New York: Theatre Arts Books, 1965], 127). Harold Jenkins comments on the speech in his "Longer Note" in the Arden edition, calling it the "supremely imaginative culmination" of "Shakespeare's conception of Ophelia." Among other things, he points out that "It is often conjectured that this *account of Ophelia's death* was inspired by that of the remarkably named Katherine Hamlett, at Tiddington, near Stratford, in December 1579. Going with a pail to fetch water from the Avon, she slipped, fell in, and was drowned. . . . There may be more than coincidence here, and although Dover Wilson robustly observes that a December drowning could hardly have supplied Shakespeare with his setting, an imagination familiar with the Avon scene could well have transposed the incident, in recalling it years later, to a less austere season" ([London and New York: Methuen, 1982], 554, 546). Elaine Showalter also mentions the speech, pointing out that "The English Pre-Raphaelites painted her again and again, choosing the drowning which is only described in the play, and where no actress's image had preceded them or interfered with their imaginative supremacy" ("Representing Ophelia: Women, Madness, and the Responsibilities of Feminist Criticism," in *Shakespeare and the Question of Theory*, ed. Patricia Parker and Geoffrey Hartman [New York and London: Methuen, 1985], 84). Philippa Berry notes in passing that "[b]oth the forms of [Ophelia's] madness and the way in which her death is described by Gertrude ally her curiously metamorphic part in this tragedy to a cognitive mode of 'conception'" (*Shakespeare's Feminine Endings* [London and New York: Routledge, 1999], 70).

3. Following the suggestions of the Ghost and Hamlet himself, many critics have argued that Gertrude committed adultery, had some part in King Hamlet's murder, or both. According to Bradley, it is "practically certain" that Gertrude "did not merely marry a second time with indecent haste; she was false to her husband while she lived. On the other hand, she was *not* privy to the murder of her husband, either before the deed or after it." Demonstrating the virtues and limitations of early twentieth-century character criticism, he goes on to say that "The Queen was not a bad-hearted woman, not at all the woman to think little of murder. But she had a soft animal nature, and was very dull and very shallow. She loved to be happy, like a sheep in the sun; and, to do her justice, it pleased her to see others happy, like more sheep in the sun. She never saw that drunkenness is disgusting till Hamlet told her so; and,

though she knew that he considered her marriage 'o'erhasty,' she was untroubled by any shame at the feelings which had led to it. It was pleasant to sit upon her throne and see smiling faces round her, and foolish and unkind in Hamlet to persist in grieving for his father instead of marrying Ophelia and making everything comfortable" (*Shakespearean Tragedy* [London: Macmillan and Company, 1957], 134–35). More recently, see Stephen Orgel's claim both that "the only Shakespearean marriage that is presented specifically as sexually happy is that of Claudius and Gertrude, the incestuous union of a murderer and an adulteress" (*Impersonations: The Performance of Gender in Shakespeare's England* [Cambridge: Cambridge University Press, 1996], 18), and that Shakespeare himself may have committed adultery, and even fathered illegitimate children: "we do not in the least know that Susanna, Hamnet and Judith were his only children. He lived in a society without contraceptives, and unless we want to believe that he was either exclusively homosexual or celibate, we must assume a high degree of probability that there were other children" ("Prospero's Wife," in *Representing the English Renaissance*, ed. Stephen Greenblatt [Berkeley: University of California Press, 1988], 223); Valerie Traub's argument that "[I]n *Hamlet*, Gertrude's adultery and incest—the uncontrollability, in short, of her sexuality—are, in Hamlet's mind, projected outward to encompass the potential of such contamination in all heterosexual liaisons. . . . Gertrude's adultery turns all women into prostitutes and all men into potential cuckolds" ("Jewels, Statues and Corpses: Containment of Female Erotic Power," in *Desire and Anxiety: Circulations of Sexuality in Shakespearean Drama* [London and New York: Routledge, 1992], 29); and Janet Adelman's more skeptical sense of "how little we know about Gertrude; even the extent of her involvement in the murder of her first husband is left unclear," and of how *Hamlet*'s "rewriting" of "the story of Cain and Abel as the story of Adam and Eve . . . accounts, I think, for Gertrude's odd position in the play, especially for its failure to specify the degree to which she is complicit in the murder" (*Suffocating Mothers: Fantasies of Maternal Origin in Shakespeare's Plays, "Hamlet" to "The Tempest"* [London and New York: Routledge, 1992], 15, 30).

Fewer critics have thought Gertrude completely innocent, whether of adultery or complicity in the death of King Hamlet or both. T. S. Eliot for example argued that "To have heightened the criminality of Gertrude would have been to provide the formula for a totally dif-

ferent emotion in Hamlet; it is just *because* her character is so negative and insignificant that she arouses in Hamlet the feeling which she
is incapable of representing" ("Hamlet," in *Selected Essays* [New York:
Harcourt, Brace, 1932], 125). See also John Dover Wilson, who states
categorically that "Some have imagined that Gertrude knew of the
murder all the time. But this is impossible" (*What Happens in Hamlet*
[Cambridge: Cambridge University Press, 1962], 252); Maynard Mack,
who is less sure: "[I]t is hard to be sure how far the queen grasps the
fact that her second husband is the murderer of her first" ("The World
of Hamlet," in *Shakespeare: Modern Essays in Criticism* [New York:
Oxford University Press, 1957], 243); and, more recently, Jacqueline
Rose, who criticizes the habit of patriarchal critics to blame Gertrude:
"[L]ike Eliot, [André] Green also gets caught in the other face of the
idealization, the inevitable accusation of Gertrude: 'Is the marriage
of Gertrude consequence or cause of the murder of Hamlet's father?
I incline towards the cause [Je pencherai pour la cause]'; and at the
end of his book he takes off on a truly wild speculation which makes
Gertrude the stake in the battle between the old Fortinbras and the
old Hamlet before the start of the play" ("Hamlet—the *Mona Lisa* of
Literature," in *Shakespeare and Gender*, ed. Deborah E. Barker and Ivo
Camps [London and New York: Verso, 1995], 115–16); and Lisa Jardine, who asks "Once it has been pointed out that Gertrude is neither
complicit in the murder of Old Hamlet, nor in any way in control of
what has happened to the throne of Denmark, what is it that has happened which makes her so dramatically culpable?" ("Afterword: What
Happens in *Hamlet?*" in *Shakespeare and Gender*, 324).

    4. See Rebecca West's claim that "There is no more bizarre aspect
of the misreading of Hamlet's character than the assumption that his
relations with Ophelia were innocent and that Ophelia was a correct and
timid virgin of exquisite sensibilities. Probably the conception would not
have lasted so long in England had it not been for the popularity of the
pre-Raphaelite picture by Sir John Millais which represents her as she
floated down the glassy stream, the weeping brook; for his model was
his friend Rossetti's bride, the correct, timid, sensitive, virginal, and tu-
bercular Miss Siddal, and she was, poor thing, especially wan during the
painting of the picture, for she was immersed in a tin bath full of water
kept warm by a lamp placed underneath, like an old-fashioned hot-water
dish. We have certainly put Ophelia into the wrong category and into

the wrong century. She was not a chaste young woman. . . . The truth is that Ophelia was a disreputable young woman: not scandalously so, but still disreputable" ("The Nature of Will," in *The Court and the Castle* [New Haven: Yale University Press, 1958]; repr. in *Hamlet* [New York: W. W. Norton, 1963], 228–29). Pointing out the play's "fascination with unseen events"—"what is hid"—Patricia Parker argues that "Rebecca West's thesis of an already unchaste Ophelia is . . . beside the point. What matters is not so much the pre- or offstage history of a single character as the play's persistent harping on opening something closed, the attempts everywhere within it to ferret out secrets and disclose what is hid. As with the possibility of the queen's adultery (or Desdemona's in *Othello*), what is at issue is fascination with unseen events, the obsession everywhere in *Hamlet* with spying and being spied upon linked with the secrets of women that can be exposed to show, a fascination that makes women, marginalized as *characters* within the play, paradoxically central to it" (*Shakespeare from the Margins* [Chicago: University of Chicago Press, 1996], 256). To Francis Berry, the spying in *Hamlet* is the cause of what he calls "Insets" (speeches that talk about unseen offstage action, action we hear about in words only): "*Hamlet* is crowded with Insets because it is full of espionage and eavesdropping. Reynaldo spies on Laertes and Polonius eavesdrops on Hamlet; Hamlet eavesdrops on the Gravediggers and the Gravediggers spy out Yorick. The theatre-audience will not watch 'The Murder of Gonzago' merely through the stage-auditor, Claudius. Rather, they will watch it through Hamlet as he watches Claudius as Claudius watches 'The Murder of Gonzago'" (*The Shakespeare Inset*, 119).

5. Shakespeare also links the word "fantastic" to the idea of grief in *Measure for Measure*, where Isabella tells Angelo how "man, proud man, . . . / Plays such fantastic tricks before high heaven / As make the angels weep" (2.2.117–22); he uses it to suggest a similar connection to madness in *Troilus and Cressida*, where Ulysses describes how "Ajax hath lost a friend, / And foams at the mouth, and he is armed and at it, / Roaring for Troilus, who hath done today / Mad and fantastic execution" (5.5.35–38).

6. A number of critics have speculated on the possibility that Gertrude was an eyewitness to Ophelia's death. Variorum cites Seymour: "As the Queen seems to give this description from ocular knowledge, it may be asked why, apprised as she was of Ophelia's distraction, she did

not take steps to prevent the fatal catastrophe, especially as there was so fair an opportunity of saving her while she was, by her clothes, borne 'mermaidlike-up,' and the Queen was at leisure to hear her 'chanting' old tunes" (373). Similarly, Philip Edwards, editor of The New Cambridge Shakespeare edition (1985) notes that "The modern reader cannot suppress his astonishment that Gertrude should have watched Ophelia die without lifting a finger to help her. Shakespeare wrote for a theatre audience before the realistic novel had come into existence: this speech is an impersonal account of Ophelia's death. It has been suggested that the queen's story is something of a 'cover up' of a deliberate act of suicide; the priest (in 5.1.194–97) says there *had* been such a cover-up. In that case, the queen's narrative becomes implausible at this point. In view of Shakespeare's total inconsistency about Horatio's awareness of life in Elsinore . . . it is better to say that Gertrude steps out of her role to serve the purpose of the play" (212). See also Francis Berry, who claims that Gertrude's speech "purport[s] to be an eye-witness account" (129).

7. See for instance "goads, thorns, nettles, tails of wasps—" (*The Winter's Tale*, 1.2.328); "Yield stinging nettles to mine enemies" (*Richard II*, 3.2.18); "out of this nettle, danger, we pluck this flower, safety" (*1 Henry IV*, 2.3.9–10); and "hemlock, nettles, cuckooflowers,/Darnel, and all the idle weeds that grow" (*King Lear*, 4.3.4–5).

8. The word "willow" appears twenty-five times in Shakespeare, sixteen of those in the song Desdemona sings to Emilia, which also has a stream, a scorned female lover, and a garland: "The poor soul sat sighing by a sycamore tree,/Sing all a green willow;/Her hand on her bosom, her head on her knee,/Sing willow, willow, willow./The fresh streams ran by her and murmured her moans;/Sing willow, willow, willow./Her salt tears fell from her, and softened the stones, / Sing willow, willow, willow" / Lay by these.—"Willow, willow." / Prithee hie thee; he'll come anon. / "Sing all a green willow must be my garland./Let nobody blame him; his scorn I approve"—/ . . . "I called my love false love, but what said he then?/Sing willow, willow, willow: If I court more women, you'll couch with more men" (*Othello*, 4.3.40–55). Daisies appear twice elsewhere in Shakespeare: "When daisies pied and violets blew" (*Love's Labors Lost*, 5.2.877) and "Let us/Find out the prettiest daisied plot we can" (*Cymbeline*, 4.2.397–98).

9. See Variorum: Farren (*Mania and Madness*) calls this line "an exquisite specimen of emblematic or picture-writing. The 'crow-

flower' . . . was called *The fayre Mayde of France*; the 'long purples' are *dead-men's-fingers*; the 'daisy' imports *pure virginity* or *spring of life*, as being itself 'the virgin bloom of the year.' The order runs thus, with the meaning of each flower beneath:

CROW-FLOWERS,	NETTLES,	DAISIES,	LONG PURPLES
Fayre Mayde	stung to	virgin	cold hand
	The quick,	bloom	of death.

'A fair maid stung to the quick, her virgin bloom under the cold hand of death.'" Steevens reports that Lyte's *Herbal* preserves "its various names, too gross for repetition"; Malone, making a similar but more pointed claim, calls it "One of the grosser names Gertrude had a particular reason to avoid,—*the rampant widow*"; Beisley simply notes that "this is the *early purple orchis*, Orchis mascula, which blossoms in April and May" (371).

    10. See *OED* 5a, which cites *long purple* and, under *long* 18c, identifies *orchis mascula* and *Lythrum Salicaria*—citing this line as the earliest example—family *Lythraceae*, commonly known as the purple loosestrife, "an extremely dominant weed, spreading widely through wetlands and overwhelming indigenous plants" (Christopher Woods, *Encyclopedia of Perennials: A Gardener's Guide* [New York and Oxford: Facts on File, 1992], 192). For other instances of the word "purple" in Shakespeare, see for example "The purple testament of bleeding war" (*Richard II*, 3.3.94); "The purple sap from her sweet brother's body" (*Richard III*, 4.4.277); "purple fountains issuing from your veins" (*Romeo and Juliet*, 1.1.84); and Oberon's description of the "little western flower,/Before milk-white, now purple with love's wound" (*A Midsummer's Night Dream*, 2.1.166–67), where Shakespeare combines both the bloody and floral associations of purple.

    11. *OED* 4b, whose example from Elyot's *Castle Helthe* [1541] refers to "swellynges under the chynne, and in England commonly purplys, measels, and small pockes."

    12. Lyte's *Herbal* (1578), for example, refers to the testicle-like tubers of the *Orchis mascula* with words like "priest's-pintle," "dog's cullions," "fool's ballocks" and "goat's cullions" (Arden, 374; *The Oxford Shakespeare: Hamlet*, ed G. R. Hibbard [Oxford and New York: Oxford University Press, 1987, 319); loose-strife is in fact a phallic-shaped flower, with "stems erect, usually 1m. or more tall; petals about 5mm long"

(John Thomas Howell, *Marin Flora: Manual of the Flowering Planats and Ferns of Marin County, California* [Berkeley, Los Angeles and London: University of California Press, 1949; 2nd ed., 1970], 196).

13. See for example William Hazlitt, writing in 1817, who calls Ophelia "a character almost too exquisitely touching to be dwelt upon. Oh rose of May, oh flower too soon faded! Her love, her madness, her death, are described with the truest touches of tenderness and pathos. It is a character which nobody but Shakespear [*sic*] could have drawn in the way that he has done, and to the conception of which there is not even the smallest approach, except in some of the old romantic ballads" (*Characters of Shakespear's Plays*, repr. in Norton Critical Edition of *Hamlet*, ed. Cyrus Hoy [New York: W. W. Norton, 1963], 168). Compare Thomas Campbell's account of Gertrude's speech, written a year later, which praises the "exquisite beauty" of this "poetical rather than dramatic" speech (n2 above).

14. According to Eric Partridge, "brook" derives from Low German "*brok*," a marsh, and Dutch "*broek*," marshy ground, and is probably from the root of English "break" and German "*brechen*"; "a break in a river bank causes a marsh, or brook" (*Origins: A Short Etymological Dictionary of Modern English* [New York: Macmillan, 1958] 61).

15. On the sexual suggestions of "clothes," "spread," and "Ophelia," see Patricia Parker: "In contrast to the 'natural modesty' of women reported in Pliny and repeated in Crooke, Ophelia, in the 'melodious lay' . . . of her drowning, floats more openly, face up, 'her clothes spread wide" . . . in lines the ear may hear, given other such Shakespearean instances, as the spreading wide of her '*close*.' . . . See also Juliet's 'Spread thy close curtain, love-performing night' (*Romeo and Juliet*, III.ii.5); and Frankie Rubinstein's *A Dictionary of Shakespeare's Sexual Puns and Their Significance* (London: Macmillan, 1984), 251, which glosses 'spread' as 'open for copulation.' In early modern English, *spread* carries the sexual sense of spreading, enlarging, or widening that makes it a synonym for *dilate*. See *OED*, *spread* (v.) 1 and 5b. On the clothes/close quibble, see [Helge] Kökeritz, *Shakespeare's Pronunciation* [New Haven: Yale University Press, 1953], 321. See also, with the F text ('her cloathes spred wide') and Q2 ('her clothes spred wide'), the text of the Q1 ('her clothes spred wide abroade'). The *O* in Ophelia also links her name with the play on *o* elsewhere in *Hamlet*. Margreta de Grazia has also suggested to me a pun on *figlia* in Q1's Ofelia" (*Shakespeare from the Margins*, 255, 366, n1). Not-

ing Jacques Lacan's claim that the etymology of Ophelia's name is "O-phallus" ("Desire and the Interpretation of Desire in *Hamlet*," in *Literature and Psychoanalysis: The Question of Reading: Otherwise*, ed. Shoshana Felman [Baltimore: Johns Hopkins University Press, 1982], 23), Elaine Showalter argues that it probably derives from the Greek for "help" or "succor," also citing Charlotte M. Younge's suggestion that it derives from *ophis*, "serpent" ("Representing Ophelia: Women, Madness, and the Responsibilities of Feminist Criticism," in *Shakespeare and the Question of Theory*, 77, 92).

16. *OED* (sb 8) cites this line as an example of *snatch* meaning "a short passage, a few words, *of* a song, etc.; a short portion, a few bars, *of* a tune."

17. Both F and Q1 give "tunes" for Q2's rarer "lauds," whose religious overtone—lauds are hymns or psalms of praise—and suggestion of pathos "tunes" does not convey. *Laudes*, the first day-hour of the Church, traditionally concludes with Psalms 148–50, which begin "Praise ye the Lord. Praise ye the Lord from the heavens: praise him in the heights" and ends, in a passage whose reference to breath is relevant to this passage, with "Let every thing that hath breath praise the Lord. Praise ye the Lord."

CHAPTER 5

1. J. L. Austin, *How To Do Things With Words*, ed. J. O. Urmson and Marina Sbisà (Cambridge, MA: Harvard University Press, 1975), 6. See also Margaret W. Ferguson's discussion of the difference between "performative" words and deeds in *Hamlet*, which argues that Hamlet's "language . . . produces a curious effect of *materializing* the word, materializing it in a way that forces us to question the distinction between literal and figurative meanings, and that also leads us to look in new ways at the word as a spoken or written phenomenon. Hamlet's verbal tactics in the early part of the play—roughly through the closet scene—constitute a rehearsal for a more disturbing kind of materializing that occurs, with increasing frequency, in the later part of the drama. This second kind of materializing pertains to the realm of deeds as well as to that of words; . . . it reminds us that all acts performed in a theater share with words the problematic status of representation. This second type of materializing might be called *performative*." Ferguson notes that Austin "notoriously seeks to exclude from his discussion the type of performa-

tive utterance that interests [her], namely that which occurs in a stage or in a literary text. Such performatives, he writes, 'will be *in a peculiar way* hollow or void," (22, Austin's italics). (*"Hamlet*: letters and spirits," in *Shakespeare and the Question of Theory*, ed. Patricia Parker and Geoffrey Hartman [New York: Methuen, 1985], 292, 306n1).

2. H. W. Janson, *History of Art* (Englewood Cliffs, N.J.: Prentice Hall, and New York: Harry N. Abrams, 1962), 292 (painting and detail of the figures in the mirror reproduced on 290). In his masterful study of the portrait, which is "the subject of what may reasonably be called the most widely known modern interpretation of a painting, Panofsky's classic reading of the panel as a depiction of a clandestine marriage," Edwin Hall points out that "the meaning of the painting has proved elusive, with opinion presently divided on exactly what the panel depicts." Thus "[i]n recent writing the Arnolfini portrait's enigmatic qualities are often taken for granted and perceived as intrinsic to the picture and even to the artist's intentions." One view claims we "never can hope to know beyond reasonable doubt, what exactly the picture shows," which is "part and parcel of the picture's perennial fascination"; another that the painting is "a visual enigma, a riddle in which nothing is as it appears to be"; a third that "[w]e can only be sure that he meant to puzzle us—meant us to enquire, to search, to *think*" (*The Arnolfini Betrothal: Medieval Marriage and the Enigma of Van Eyck's Double Portrait* [Berkeley: University of California Press, 1994], xvii–xviii). I take these views to shed some light on the "perennial fascination" not only of van Eyck's painting but of Shakespeare's *Hamlet* as well.

3. A number of recent critics have noted the sexual implications of this exchange between Hamlet and Ophelia. See, for example, Philip Armstrong, who notes that "*Hamlet* . . . repeatedly gestures towards 'nothing', a recurrent lacuna central to the 'round O' of the Elizabethan theatre. Hamlet locates this lack between Ophelia's legs, precisely in the position from which he will observe Claudius's response to the play: . . . 'Lady, shall I lie in your lap?'. . . . To the Elizabethan audience, this exchange involves a series of sexual puns ('lie', 'head', 'country', 'no thing'), according to which, just as in the Freudian psychoanalytic account, gender difference resolves into the absence or presence of the penis. The unease surrounding this component lacking from the visual field displays all the characteristics of the Lacanian 'real'" ("Watching *Hamlet* watching: Lacan, Shakespeare and the mirror/

stage," in *Alternative Shakespeares*, vol. 2, ed. Terence Hawkes [London and New York: Routledge, 1996], 231–32); William C. Carroll, who claims that "The pun and its inversions, the malapropism, permit the introduction into utterance of female sexuality without ever seeming to name or recognize it. The references . . . may be sinister—as in the references to 'country matters' . . . in *Hamlet*" ("The Virgin Not: Language and Sexuality in Shakespeare," in *Shakespeare and Gender: A History*, ed. Deborah E Barker and Ivo Kamps [London and New York: Verso, 1995], 284); Malcolm Evans, who thinks "the 'nothing' which Ophelia 'thinks' as an epitome of the feminine—and which is 'a fair thought to lie between a maid's legs,' a genital delirium of presence and absence as she/he waits for the entrance of a fellow boy-actor who performs the part of a boy-actor representing the Player Queen" ("Deconstructing Shakespeare's Comedies," in *Alternative Shakespeares*, vol. 2, 69); David Leverenz, who notes that Hamlet's "crude jokes about 'country matters' . . . as he lies in her lap, at the play, toy with her role as honorable daughter, confirm his lust, yet contradict the piteous picture he makes of himself in her room, wordless, his clothes in disarray. His oscillating acts of need and aggression are Hamlet's nasty mirroring of what he perceives to be her mixed signals to him: her loving talks, then her inexplicable denial and silence" ("The Women in Hamlet: An Interpersonal View," in *Representing Shakespeare: New Psychoanalytic Essays*, ed. Murray M. Schwartz and Coppélia Kahn [Baltimore: Johns Hopkins University Press, 1980], 119); Patricia Parker, who argues that Hamlet's question "is made more bawdy by the reference in both Folio and Second Quarto to 'country matters,' obscenely invoking a female 'matter,' *count* or 'cunt,' and the 'nothing' that lies 'between maids' legs'" ("*Othello* and *Hamlet*: Spying, Discovery, Secret Faults," in *Shakespeare from the Margins: Language, Culture, Context* [Chicago and London: University of Chicago Press, 1996], 253); Elaine Showalter, who points out that "In Elizabethan slang, 'nothing' was a term for the female genitalia. . . . To Hamlet, then, 'nothing' is what lies between maids' legs, for, in the male visual system of representation and desire, women's sexual organs, in the words of the French psychoanalyst Luce Irigaray, 'represent the horror of having nothing to see'" ("Representing Ophelia: Woman, Madness, and the Responsibilities of Feminist Criticism," in *Shakespeare & the Question of Theory*, ed. Patricia Parker and Geoffrey Hartman [New York and London: Methuen,

1995], 79); and David Willbern, who calls *"no thing*—the sense which Hamlet intends in his notorious joking with Ophelia just before the play-within-the-play (his byplay is verbal foreplay)" ("Shakespeare's Nothing," in *Representing Shakespeare*, 245).

4. See A. C. Bradley's discussion of when Hamlet might have been seeing Ophelia, which begins with a question about the words "of late": "We are twice told that Hamlet has *'of late'* been seeking the society of Ophelia and protesting his love for her (i.iii.91, 99). It always seemed to me, on the usual view of the chronology, rather difficult (though not, of course, impossible) to understand this, considering the state of feeling produced in him by his mother's marriage, and in particular the shock it appears to have given to his faith in woman. But if the marriage has only just been celebrated the words 'of late' would naturally refer to a time before it. This time presumably would be subsequent to the death of Hamlet's father, but it is not so hard to fancy that Hamlet may have sought relief from mere *grief* in his love for Ophelia.

But here another question rises: May not the words 'of late' include, or even wholly refer to, a time prior to the death of Hamlet's father? And this question would be answered universally, I suppose, in the negative, on the ground that Hamlet was not at Court but at Wittenberg when his father died. I will deal with this idea in a separate note, and will only add here that, though it is quite possible that Shakespeare never imagined any of these matters clearly, and so produced these unimportant difficulties, we ought not to assume this without examination" (*Shakespearean Tragedy* [London: Macmillan, 1957], 340).

5. Many critics of *Hamlet* have commented on the exchange between Hamlet and Ophelia in the play scene. To take some earlier examples: Coleridge points out that "the penetrating Ham[let] perceives, from the strange and forced manner of Oph[elia], that the sweet girl was not acting a part of her own, but was a decoy; and his after-speeches are not so much directed to her as to the listeners and spies" (*A New Variorum Edition of Shakespeare: Hamlet*, ed. Horace Howard Furness [New York: J. B. Lippincott, 1877; repr. New York: Dover Publications, 1963], 216–17); in his 1870 edition, Charles Lamb reports that "All the Hamlet's that I have ever seen, rant and rave at Oph[elia] as if she had committed some great crime, and the audience are highly pleased, because the words of the part are satirical, and they are enforced by the strangest expression of satirical indignation of which the face and voice are capable. But

then, whether Ham[let] is likely to have put on such brutal appearances to a lady whom he loved so dearly, is never thought on" (Variorum, 217); Bradley, writing in 1904, points out "the disgusting and insulting grossness" of Hamlet's language (82); in 1930, G. Wilson Knight claims "Hamlet denies the existence of romantic values. Love, in his mind, has become synonymous with sex, and sex with uncleanness. Therefore beauty is dangerous and unclean. Sick of the world, of man, of love, Hamlet denies the reality of his past romance: 'I loved you not'" ("The Embassy of Death: An Essay on *Hamlet*," in *The Wheel of Fire* [London: Methuen, 1961], 25). More recently, in addition to the examples cited above (n3), Joel Fineman points out that "In *Hamlet* all women are prostitutes, and they are Hamlet-like to the extent that all of them are by nature in disguise. Because it is axiomatic that beauty transforms honesty into a bawd (III.i.110–13), it follows as a logical consequence that Hamlet, who is 'indifferent honest,' goes mad when confronted with the spectacle of dissembling woman: 'God hath given you one face, and you make yourselves another . . . it hath made me mad' (III.i.143–46)" ("Fratricide and Cuckoldry: Shakespeare's Doubles," in *Representing Shakespeare*, 81); Richard P. Wheeler writes that "The lack of direct response to Hamlet's outrageousness goes with the assumption that he is mad or deranged. Ophelia, who does not know how deeply his jilting has hurt her until she goes mad, says 'O, help him, you sweet heavens!' and finally, 'O, what a noble mind is here o'erthrown!'" (*The Whole Journey: Shakespeare's Powers of Development* [Berkeley: University of California Press, 1986], 258); Jacqueline Rose notes that "In *Hamlet*, we have seen that the breakdown of the carefully contrived sexual dichotomy (wherein virgin and whore are mutually exclusive terms) unleashes Hamlet's aggression toward Gertrude and Ophelia" (*Desire and Anxiety: Circulations of Sexuality in Shakespearean Drama* [London and New York: Routledge, 1992], 34); Janet Adelman argues that "Ophelia fuses with Gertrude not only as potential cuckold-maker but also as potential mother: 'Get thee to a nunnery. . . .' The implicit logic is: why would you be a breeder of sinners like me? In the gap between 'breeder of sinners' and 'I,' Gertrude and Ophelia momentarily collapse into one figure. It is no wonder that there can be no more marriage: Ophelia becomes dangerous to Hamlet insofar as she becomes identified in his mind with the contaminating maternal body, the mother who has borne him" (*Suffocating Mothers: Fantasies of Maternal Origin in Shakespeare's*

Plays, "Hamlet" to "The Tempest" [London and New York: Routledge, 1992], 14); and Philippa Berry argues that "It seems that Ophelia has indeed 'conceived' or understood the cryptic as well as bawdy utterances of her former suitor, after his 'words of so sweet breath' have been disturbingly replaced by a different vocal music, 'like sweet bells jangled out of tune and harsh'—a sounding of corruption and death. The metaphysical 'nothing' of which this new Hamlet speaks is also, of course, 'a fair thought to lie between maids' legs' (3.2.117). It seems, therefore, that an obscure form of cognitive insemination does occur" (*Shakespeare's Feminine Endings* [London and New York: Routledge, 1999], 70).

6. Jardine is, as far as I know, the only critic to call attention to the possibility that Hamlet and Ophelia may have had sex in Ophelia's closet: "Because what goes on in the closet is—uniquely amongst the activities in the early modern gentrified household—customarily solitary, a suggestion of the illicit, indiscreet, certainly the secretive, hovers over those infrequent occasions when men and women encounter one another there, a *frisson* of likely indiscretion audible in Ophelia's anxious account of Hamlet's intrusion 'all unbrac'd' into her private quarters in Act II, Scene i. For beyond Hamlet's disheveled appearance, his very entry into the entirely unsupervised, solitary intimacy of Ophelia's closet suggests an erotic entanglement" ("Afterword: What Happens in *Hamlet*," in *Shakespeare and Gender*, 318–19). Probably without meaning to, Bradley suggests something of the same thing when he asks, "When Hamlet made his way into Ophelia's room, why did he go in the garb, the conventionally recognized garb, of the distracted *lover?*" (125). More recently, John Updike has also imagined that Hamlet and Ophelia have been sexually active: "The King wondered about the sleeplessness that set such a pallor on [Hamlet's] face—up till the russet dawn with Ophelia, sullying his flesh? She was not here, still abed: a novice slut" (*Gertrude and Claudius* [New York: Alfred A. Knopf, 2000], 206).

7. The physical "remembrances" in 3.1 are one of several props in the play, others being the pikes and lances carried by Barnardo, Francisco, and Marcellus in the opening scene; the paper on which Claudius has written "this greeting to Old Norway" (1.2.35); Hamlet's sword on which he wants Horatio and Marcellus to "swear" 1.5.157, 62); "this money and these notes" (2.1.1) that Polonius gives to Reynaldo (to be given to Laertes); various written texts in 2.2—the request by Fortinbras that he be allowed to pass across Denmark, delivered by Voltemand to

the King, followed by Hamlet's letter to Ophelia, read by Polonius to the King and Queen, and Hamlet's book; another book that Polonius gives to Ophelia to read when he sends her to entrap Hamlet in 3.1; the crown, the vial of poison, and various "gifts" with which the "poisoner woos the Queen" in the dumb show in 3.2; recorders that Hamlet banters with Rosencrantz and Guildenstern about in 3.2; the sword with which Hamlet stabs Polonius through the arras in 3.4 as well as the two lockets with pictures of "[t]he counterfeit presentment of two brothers" (3.4.54) that he shows to his mother in the same scene; the flowers—"rosemary" (4.4.170), "pansies" (171), "fennel" (175), "columbines" (175), "rue" (176), "a daisy" 178)—that Ophelia gives to Claudius, Gertrude, and Laertes; Hamlet's two letters announcing his return to Denmark in 4.7, one of which is read by Horatio and the other by Claudius; the various skulls in 5.1 as well as what the priest calls Ophelia's "virgin crants, / Her maiden strewments" (221–22); and last but not least the "Trumpets, Drums . . . cushions . . . *foils, daggers*" noted in the stage direction of the final scene. In each instance, the play tells us, if not explicitly then by quite explicit suggestion, exactly what the physical object held or lifted or read or thrown or drunk actually is.

8. The prompt books for these five RSC performances were made available to members of the Shakespeare Association of America Workshop on "Teaching through Performance: *Hamlet*, 3.1," held in Miami on April 14, 2001. The Workshop was lead by Miriam Gilbert, to whom I am grateful for making available copies of the RSC promptbooks from these productions. A survey of film productions would yield similar results; compare for example Olivier's 1948 film production of *Hamlet*, in which Ophelia pulls something from the bosom of her long white nightgown-like dress on the lines "My Lord, I have remembrances of yours / That I have longèd long to redeliver" (3.1.93–94), holds them in her hand (we cannot quite see what they are—crumpled flowers? beads on a cloth, a handkerchief?), then puts them on a stone stand beside her on the line "Rich gifts prove poor when givers prove unkind. There, my Lord" (101–2). At which point he puts his hand over hers and asks, "Are you honest" (103). Elsewhere, asking what Ophelia's "tenders of [Hamlet's] affections" (1.3.98–99) might be, Gilbert also notes that "An earlier play, *A Midsummer's Night's Dream*, offers us a detailed list of a lover's tokens as Egeus angrily catalogues the gifts to his daughter Hermia from her suitor Lysander: 'bracelets of thy hair, rings, gauds,

conceits, / Knacks, trifles, nosegays, sweetmeats' (1.1.33–34). In *The Winter's Tale*, Autolycus's song offers a range of gifts 'for my lads to give their dears,' including fabrics, masks, and jewellery, while in *Love's Labour's Lost*, the male lovers send the women they are wooing even more upscale gifts of gloves, pearls, and diamonds along with their love-verses" ("Performance Criticism," in *Shakespeare: An Oxford Guide*, ed. Stanley Wells and Lena Cowen Orlin [Oxford: Oxford University Press, 2003)] 556).

9. See Stephen Booth, "Close readers who want their prospective clients to accept readings that derive from some previously unobserved potential in a line are always at risk of being laughed at for wanton ingenuity" ("Close Reading without Readings," in *Shakespeare Reread: The Text in New Contexts*, ed. Russ McDonald [Ithaca, NY: Cornell University Press, 1994], 43).

10. The name "Ophelia" combines "O" (zero, Ophelia's "nothing") with the Greek root for love ("philos"), which sounds like "phallus," suggesting not only love itself but both the female and the male sex organ. See David Willbern's discussion of the significance of "O"—"the sign of nothing, the sound of nothing" ("Shakespeare's Nothing," in *Representing Shakespeare* [Baltimore, MD: Johns Hopkins University Press, 1980], 244–63). For further discussion of Ophelia's name, see Chapter 4, n15.

11. Under "nymph," *OED* gives an example from *A Midsummer Night's Dream* 4.1.124 ("But soft! What nymphs are these? *Egeus*. My Lord, this is my daughter here asleep."); under "Nympha," which derives from Greek *nymphae* for bride or nymph and whose anatomical meaning is "the labia minora of the vulva, situated within the labia majora"), an example from the 2nd edition of *Blancard's Psyc. Dict* ("*Nymphae*, little pieces of Flesh in a Woman's Secrets"). Although this earliest known example is from 1693, it seems likely that such a meaning would have also been available to Shakespeare, especially considering the context in which he uses it here. Shakespeare suggests the potentially sexual meaning of nymph in *The Tempest* 4.1.65–66 ("Which spongy April at thy hest betrims, / To make cold nymphs chaste crowns"), *A Midsummer Night's Dream* 2.1.245–46 ("Fare thee well, nymph. Ere he do leave this grove, / Thou shalt fly him, and he shall seek thy love"); and *Richard III* 1.1.16–17 ("and want love's majesty / To strut before a wanton ambling nymph").

12. *OED* sb.3, which cites *The Tempest* 1.2.347–48 as an example ("till thou didst seek to violate / The honor of my child"). For other examples

of "honor" used in a sexual sense, see *Much Ado About Nothing* 4.1.191–92 ("If they wrong her honor,/The proudest of them shall well hear of it") and 300–1 ("Is a not approved in the height a villain, that hath slandered, scorned, dishonored my kinswoman?"), *Twelfth Night* 3.1.149 ("By maidhood, honor, truth and everything"), *The Winter's Tale* 2.1.159–60 ("more it would content me/To have her honor true than your suspicion"), 2.2.9–11 ("Here's ado,/To lock up honor and honesty from/Th' access of gentle visitors") and 43 ("Your honor and your goodness is so evident").

13. For the potentially sexual meaning of "well," see Stephen Booth, *Shakespeare's Sonnets* (New Haven and London: Yale University Press, 1977): 129.13 ("if Shakespeare's reader were accustomed to hearing . . . the female sex organ called a *well*") and 154.9 ("*well* is probably intended . . . as a bawdy metaphor for the female sex organ"); Booth cites *All's Well that Ends Well* 1.1.152–70 as a further example. For the phonetic likeness and bawdy punning on "well" and "will," see notes on 112.3 and 135, headnote.

14. *OED* v.3, which defines "deliver" as "To disburden (a woman) *of* the foetus, to bring to childbirth"), cites *The Winter's Tale* 2.2.25 as an example ("She is something before her time delivered"). Shakespeare uses this meaning of "deliver" elsewhere, for example in *Titus Andronicus* 4.2.61 "She is delivered, lords, she is delivered."), 4.2.141–42 ("The midwife and myself, And no one else but the delivered empress"), and 5.3.119–20 ("Behold the child: Of this was Tamora deliverèd"); *Othello* 1.3.377–78 ("There are many events in the womb of time which will be delivered") and 2.1.127–28 ("my muse labors,/And thus she is delivered"); and *Henry VIII* 5.1.162 ("Is the Queen delivered?/Say ay, and of a boy").

15. For the potential of sexual meaning in "aught," a pronoun meaning "Anything whatever, anything" (*OED* A, derived from "OE *á, ó*, ever + *whit* creature, being, wight, whit, *thing*" [italics mine]), see Booth's note on Sonnet 21.12: "*thing* . . . (2) generative organ (used both for 'penis' [as in *Lear* I.5.49; see Florio, s.v., *cotale*] and for 'vulva' [see *2Gent* III.i.340–43; Florio glosses *cotalina* as 'a little pretty thing or quaint']. . . . 'Nothing' and 'naught' were popular cant terms for 'vulva' [perhaps because of the shape of the zero]; compare the use of *nothing* in *Ham* III.ii.105–16 [the 'country matters' passage]"). Booth also cites Thomas Pyles, "Ophelia's Nothing," *MLN*, XLIV (May 1949, 322–23, and Paul Jorgensen, "Much

Ado About *Nothing*," *SQ*, V.3 (Summer 1954) 287–95. For the sexual suggestion of "aught" meaning "nothing," see David Willbern's account of "Nothing/Zero/Cipher": "'These mathematical terms include various synonyms of 'nothing' such as 'nil,' 'null,' 'none,' 'naught' ('nought'), and 'aught' ('ought'). 'Zero' and 'cipher' share the same Arabic root: *sifr*, meaning 'empty.' The two meanings of 'cipher' convey the primary dialectic of presence and absence. As a synonym for zero, it means 'empty,' 'nothing'; it also means 'secret letter' or 'code' (it signifies the absence of a specific and salient presence). Nothing by itself, in context its meanings are multiple, like Polixenes' 'cipher . . . standing in rich place'" (252).

16. See *OED* 5, which gives *The Winter's Tale* 5.1.83 as an example ("when your first queen's again in breath"). For the possibility of sexual meanings in "spirit," see Booth's extended note on Sonnet 129.1.

17. *OED* sb.6, which cites this line as an example; the Pelican edition also glosses "commerce" in line 109 as "intercourse."

18. See for example the vaguely suggestive sexual associations in *Romeo and Juliet* 3.2.134–35 ("He made you [the rope] for a highway to my bed;/But I, a maid, die maiden-widowèd"), *Twelfth Night* 3.4.49–50 (Malvolio: "Go to, thou art made, if thou desir'st to be so." Olivia: "Am I made?"), *Measure for Measure* 3.2.98–101 ("They say this Angelo was not made by man and woman after this downright way of creation. . . . How should he be made then?"), and *Othello* 1.1.115–16 ("your daughter and the Moor are making the beast with two backs") and 2.3.15–16 ("He hath not yet made wanton the night with her").

19. For similar instances of "stock" meaning lineage in Shakespeare, see *The Merchant of Venice* 4.1.294–95 ("Would any of the stock of Barrabas/Had been her husband"), *Henry V* 1.2.71 ("Of the true line and stock of Charles the Great"), and *Cymbeline* 1.6.126–28 ("Be revenged,/Or she that bore you was no queen, and you/Recoil from your great stock").

20. See G. Wilson Knight's comment on this speech, which suggests—though he probably does not intend to—the possibility that Hamlet and Ophelia have had sex: "Hamlet denies the existence of romantic values. Love, in his mind, has become synonymous with sex, and sex with uncleanness. Therefore beauty is dangerous and unclean. Sick of the world, of man, of love, Hamlet denies the reality of his past romance: 'I loved you not'" ("The Embassy of Death: An Essay on *Hamlet*," in *The Wheel of Fire* [London: Methuen, 1961], 25).

21. For nunnery as brothel or house of ill fame, *OED* cites one exam-

ple in 1593 from Nashe's *Christ's Tears* ("To Some one Gentleman generally acquanted, they give . . . free priviledge thenceforward in theyr Nunnery to procure them frequentence") and another in 1617 from Fletcher's *The Mad Lover* ("There's an old Nunerie at hand. What's that? A bawdy-house."). Harold Jenkins's note on this line in Arden questions the relevance of this meaning to this passage, claiming that "to insist on [this meaning] (as in [John Dover Wilson's *What Happens in Hamlet*] pp. 128–34) at the expense of the literal meaning, itself so poignant in the context, is perverse" ([London and New York: Methuen, 1982], 282). In his "Longer Note" on "a nunnery" (493–96), Jenkins discusses both of the *OED*'s examples of the "naughty meaning" of "nunnery" as well as other possible instances of this meaning, including the German play *Tragaedia der Bestrafte Bredermord oder Prinz Hamlet aus Dännemark*, which was performed by an English troupe at Dresden in 1626 and includes Hamlet's command to Ophelia to "go to a nunnery, but not to a nunnery where two pairs of slippers lie at the bedside"), which thus, as Jenkins puts it, "confirms what a 17th-century 'nunnery' could be." In the end, Jenkins seems to admit that the word would have most likely conveyed both of its contrary senses simultaneously.

22. David Leverenz points out "Robin is a colloquial Elizabethan term for penis" ("The Woman in Hamlet: An Interpersonal View," in *Representing Shakespeare*, 120). See also Harry Morris, "Ophelia's 'Bonny Sweet Robin,'" *PMLA*, 73 (1958), 601–3; and Carroll Camden, "On Ophelia's Madness," *Shakespeare Quarterly* 15 (1964), 247–55.

23. Noting the play's pervasive concern with "show and tell, eye and ear," Patricia Parker sees Polonius hidden behind the arras as part of a "network of informers and spies" which is "everywhere in *Hamlet*, adding to the claustrophobia that pervades the world of the play. . . . The play on show and tell, eye and ear, exploited in *The Mousetrap* scene echoes throughout in these dual modalities of 'informing.' Spying with the eye and ferreting out a narrative are combined within the closet scene, where Polonius, come as spy, hides behind the arras in order to 'hear' the 'process' (in early modern English, 'narrative') of what transpires" (257).

24. Stephen Greenblatt points out that "The closet scene is the last time that Hamlet—or the audience—sees the spirit of his father. It has already in some sense started to vanish. In the first act, though it spoke only to Hamlet, the Ghost was seen by Horatio, Marcellus, and Barnardo; now Hamlet seems to his mother to be bending his 'eye on va-

cancy' and talking to 'th'incorporal air' (3.4.108–9)" (*Hamlet in Purgatory* [Princeton: Princeton University Press, 2001], 225).

25. See Norman Holland's discussion of psychoanalytic readings of *Hamlet* from Freud through 1969 in *Psychoanalysis and Shakespeare* (New York: Octagon Books, 1976), 163–206; also David Willbern's "Bibliography of Psychoanalytic and Psychological Writings on Shakespeare: 1964–1978," in *Representing Shakespeare*, 264–86.

26. A number of critics have mentioned what Patricia Parker calls "the tortured syntax" of this speech. Parker notes the link between "matter" and "mother" (*mater*), made explicit both in Hamlet's "but to the matter: my mother" (3.2.311), when Rosencrantz tells him that his mother "wants to speak with [him] in her closet ere [he goes] to bed" (317–18) and in his "Now, mother, what's the matter" (3.4.9), and "even more strikingly suggested in the tortured syntax of Hamlet's desire that his mother not 'ravel' a secret 'matter' out" (254). Adelman claims that "Here, as in the play within the play, Hamlet recreates obsessively, voyeuristically, the acts that have corrupted the royal bed, even when he has to subject his logic and syntax to considerable strain to do so. . . . There has to be an easier way of asking your mother not to reveal that your madness is an act" (32). For further discussion of "mother"/"mater," see Ferguson, who notes that "matter" appears 26 times in *Hamlet*, more than in any other play by Shakespeare, and that "As we hear or see in the word 'matter' the Latin term for mother, we may surmise that the common Renaissance association between female nature in general and the 'lower' realm of matter is here being deployed in the service of Hamlet's complex oedipal struggle. The mother is the matter that comes between the father and the son—and it is no accident that in this closet scene Hamlet's sexual hysteria rises to its highest pitch" (294–95); and Adelman, who argues that "matter itself is the diseased inheritance of the female body: the myth that made Eve responsible for the Fall and hence for the mortal body is played out in miniature in any ordinary birth" (6).

27. Adelman claims that "Gertrude is the only fully sexualized female body in the play, and we experience her sexuality largely through the imagination of her son" and that "Hamlet cannot stop imagining, even commanding, the sexual act that he wants to undo" (27, 32).

28. On Hamlet and Claudius as "mighty opposites," see Hawkes: "Claudius ceases to be the simple stage-villain described by the Ghost

and required by the smoothing-over process of interpretation that linear progressions demands. He has many more than one role, and these are complex, manifold: he is brother (even the primal brother, Cain, as he himself suggests), father in a legal and political sense to Hamlet, lover and later husband to Gertrude, murderer of King Hamlet, monarchy, and political head of the state. In a sense, all these roles are situated within his enormously forceful role of uncle, on the basis of which his opposition to Hamlet is determined. He is, as the play terms him, no simple villain, but Hamlet's 'mighty opposite'" (317). Likewise, several critics have noted Hamlet's resemblance to Claudius. See for example Ernest Jones's claim in his classic oedipal reading of the play: "his own 'evil' prevents [Hamlet] from completely denouncing his uncle's, and in continuing to 'repress' the former he must strive to ignore, to condone, and if possible even to forget the latter; *his moral fate is bound up with his uncle's for good or ill.* In reality his uncle incorporates the deepest and most buried part of his own personality." Hamlet's "uncle incorporates the deepest and most buried part of his own personality, so that he cannot kill him without also killing himself" (*Hamlet and Oedipus* [Garden City, NY: Doubleday, 1949], 100); Joel Fineman's account of what he calls Freud and Jones's "'psychological' reading: Claudius with his villainy acts out Hamlet's oedipal desire and in doing so both stimulates and frustrates Hamlet's oedipal will. . . . [B]y raising himself to the place of Hamlet's father, Claudius at the same time raises Hamlet to what formerly was Claudius' own place. In other words, for the characters in the play, as for the audience that perceives them, Hamlet becomes Claudius' brother when Claudius becomes Hamlet's father, which is what makes them, as Hamlet defines their relation in his first words, 'A little more than kin, and less than kind!' (I.ii.65), and which explains the inverted self-regard with which uncle and nephew measure each other by reference to the ambiguity of 'our sometime sister, now our queen' (I.ii.8)" ("Fratricide and Cuckoldry: Shakespeare's Doubles," in *Representing Shakespeare*, 76); Janet Adelman's argument that "As his memory of his father pushes increasingly in the direction of idealization, Hamlet becomes more acutely aware of his own distance from that idealization and hence of his likeness to Claudius" (13); and Margaret W. Ferguson's claim that "[i]n coming to resemble Claudius, Hamlet is driven to forget this distinction [between "[u]nyoking words from their conventional meanings" and "unyoking bodies from spirits"] ("*Hamlet*: letters and spirits," in *Shakespeare and the Question of Theory*, 300).

29. Shakespeare also uses "mouse" as a term of endearment in *Love's Labors Lost* ("What's your dark meaning, mouse, of this light word" [5.2.19]) and *Twelfth Night* ("Good my mouse of virtue, answer me" [1.5.58–59]). Although Shakespeare uses "wanton" frequently as an adjective of persons (as in *King Lear* 4.1.37–38, "As flies to wanton boys are we to th' gods;/They kill us for their sport") or things (as in *A Midsummer Night's Dream* 2.1.128–29, "When we have laughed to see the sails conceive/And grow big-bellied with the wanton wind") or even nature (as in *A Midsummer Night's Dream* 2.1.99–100, "And the quaint mazes in the wanton green/For lack of tread are indistinguishable"), as a noun of persons (as in *Much Ado About Nothing* 4.1.42–43, "Not to be married,/Not to knit my soul to an approvèd wanton") or *Othello* 4.1.70–72, "O, 'tis the spite of hell, the fiend's arch-mock,/To lip a wanton in a secure couch,/And to suppose her chaste!"), and as a verb (as in *Titus Andronicus* 2.1.21, "to wanton with this queen" and *The Winter's Tale* 2.1.16–18, "We shall/Present our services to a fine new prince/One of these days, and then you'd wanton with us"), it seems to function here as a noun of the action being performed "to pinch or play wanton," as it does in *Richard II* 3.3.164, "Or shall we play the wantons with our woes."

30. The *OED* defines "reechy" as "smokey, squalid, dirty, rancid," citing the two other instances of it in Shakespeare: *Much Ado About Nothing* 3.3.134–35, "Like Pharaoh's soldiers in the reechy painting," and, with similar reference to the body, *Coriolanus* 2.1.203–4, "the kitchen malkin pins/Her richest lockram 'bout her reechy neck." Suggesting the animal overtones of "reechy," Variorum cites Dyce: "Reechy is greasy, sweaty. . . . Laneham, speaking of 'three pretty puzels' in a morris-dance, says they were '*az* bright az a breast of bacon,' that is, bacon hung in the *chimney*; and hence *reechy*, which in its primitive signification is *smoky*, came to imply greasy"; and Clarendon: "In the present passage the word may have been suggested by 'bloat,' two lines before, which has also the meaning 'to cure herrings by hanging them in the smoke'" (306)

31. *OED* cites this line as an example of "paddle" as an intransitive verb, meaning "To play or dabble idly or fondly (*in, on, with,* or *about* something) with the fingers, to toy," as well as *Othello* 2.1.251–52 ("Didst

thou not see her paddle with the palm of his hand"); and as a transitive verb, meaning "To finger idly, playfully, or fondly," cites *The Winter's Tale* 1.2.115 ("to be paddling palms, and pinching fingers,/As now they are, and making practiced smiles/As in a looking glass").

32. Bradley, 123

AFTERWORD

1. The most recent biography of Shakespeare is Stephen Greenblatt's excellent (and best-selling) *Will in the World* (New York: W. W. Norton, 2004). See also Katherine Duncan Jones, *Ungentle Shakespeare: Scenes from His Life* (London: Arden Shakespeare, 2001), Park Honan, *Shakespeare: A Life* (Oxford: Oxford University Press, 1998), and Jonathan Bate, *The Genius of Shakespeare* (London: Picador, 1997). For recent accounts of the authorship controversy, see Marjorie Garber, "Shakespeare's Ghost Writers," *Shakespeare's Ghost Writers: Literature as Uncanny Causality* (New York and London: Methuen, 1987), 1–12; Samuel Schoenbaum, *Shakespeare's Lives* (New York: Oxford University Press, 1991), 381–451; and Richard Levin, "The Poetics and Politics of Bardicide," *PMLA* 105 (1990): 491–504. For a biased account of the Oxfordian claim in particular, see Charleton Ogburn, *The Mysterious William Shakespeare* (McLean, Virginia: EPM Publications, 1984). For a detailed discussion of the title page and frontispiece of the First Folio, and of the universality versus localization of Shakespeare and his art, see Leah Marcus, *Puzzling Shakespeare* (Berkeley: University of California Press, 1988), 1–50. For an account of the publication history of Shakespeare's plays both in quartos and the 1623 Folio, and of Shakespeare's "lack of interest in print publication," see David Scott Kastan, "Shakespeare in Print," in *Shakespeare After Theory* (New York and London: Routledge, 1999), 71–92.

2. "Words of the fragrant portals, dimly-starred,/And of ourselves and of our origins,/In ghostlier demarcations, keener sounds." Wallace Stevens, "The Idea of Order at Key West," in *The Collected Poems of Wallace Stevens* (New York: Alfred A. Knopf, 1954), 130. See also Garber's claim about the relation between Shakespeare and the Ghost in *Hamlet*: "If anything is clear, it is that the Ghost is not—or not merely—Shakespeare *père* or Shakespeare *fils*, the son of John Shakespeare or the father of Hamnet—but rather 'Shakespeare' itself. . . . The Ghost is Shakespeare. He is the one who comes as a revenant, belatedly instated, regarded as originally authoritative, rather than retrospectively

and retroactively canonized, and deriving increased authority from this very instatement of authority backward, over time. . . . 'Remember me!' cries the Ghost, and Shakespeare is for us the superego of literature, that which calls us back to ourselves, to an imposed undecidable, but self-chosen attribution of paternity. 'Remember me!' The canon has been fixed against self-slaughter" (175–76). Looking at historical evidence, Greenblatt speculates that Shakespeare's father is the spirit behind *Hamlet*'s ghost: "When in 1757, the owner of Shakespeare's birthplace in Stratford-upon-Avon decided to retile the roof, one of the workmen, described as of 'very honest, sober, and industrious character,' found an old document between the rafters and the tiling. The document, six leaves stitched together, was a 'spiritual testament' in fourteen articles . . . conspicuously Catholic in content; written by the celebrated Italian priest Carlo Borromeo, . . . translated, smuggled into England by Jesuits, and distributed to the faithful. If genuine (for the original has disappeared), the copy discovered in Stratford belonged to John Shakespeare. In it the devout Catholic acknowledges that he is mortal and born to die 'without knowing the hour, where, when, or how.' Fearing that he may be 'surprised upon a sudden,' the signer of the testament declares his pious intention to receive at his death the sacraments of confession, Mass, and extreme unction. If by some terrible 'accident' he does not receive these sacraments (that is, if he dies 'unhouseled, dis-appointed, ananeled'), then he wishes God to pardon him. His appeal for spiritual assistance is not only to God, the blessed Virgin, and his guardian angel, it is also to his family: 'I John Shakespeare,' reads article XII, 'do in like manner pray and beseech all my dear friends, Parents, and kinsfolks, by the bowels of our Savior Jesus Christ, that since it is uncertain what lot will befall me, for fear notwithstanding lest by reason of my sins, I be to pass, and stay a long while in Purgatory, they will vouchsafe to assist and succor me with their holy prayers, and satisfactory works, especially with the holy Sacrifice of the Mass, as being the most effectual means to deliver souls from their torments and pains; from the which, if I shall by God's gracious goodness, and by their virtuous works be delivered, I do promise that I will not be ungrateful unto them, for so great a benefit.' There is a clear implication to be drawn from this document: the playwright was probably brought up in a Roman Catholic household in a time of official suspicion and persecution of recusancy. And there is . . . a further implication, particularly if we take seriously the evidence that

Shakespeare conformed to the Church of England: in 1601 the Protestant playwright was haunted by the spirit of his Catholic father pleading for suffrages to relieve his soul from the pains of Purgatory" (*Hamlet in Purgatory* [Princeton: Princeton University Press, 2001], 248–49).

3. Speculation about the relation between Shakespeare's *Hamlet* and Shakespeare's life has been widespread. See for example Freud's claim (published in 1900) that *Hamlet* "was composed immediately after the death of Shakespeare's father (1601)—that is to say, when he was still mourning his loss, and during a revival, as we may fairly assume, of his own childish feelings in respect of his father. It is known, too, that Shakespeare's son, who died in childhood, bore the name of Hamnet (identical with Hamlet)" ("The Interpretation of Dreams," in *The Basic Writings of Sigmund Freud*, ed. and trans. A. A. Brill [New York: Random House, 1966], 310); Harold C. Goddard's less certain but similar claim that "To nearly everyone both Hamlet himself and the play give the impression of having some peculiarly intimate relation to their creator. What that relation may originally have been we shall probably never know. But it is hard to refrain from speculating. . . . Shakespeare's son Hamnet died at the age of eleven, possibly not long before his father began to be attracted by the Hamlet story. Was there any connection? We do not know. . . . Hamnet and Judith Sadler, neighbors and friends of the Shakespeares, were godparents to their twins, to whom they gave their names. When Shakespeare was sixteen, a girl, Katherine Hamlett, was drowned near Stratford under circumstances the poet may have remembered when he told of Ophelia's death" (*The Meaning of Shakespeare*, vol. 1 [Chicago: University of Chicago Press, 1951], 332); and, most recently, Greenblatt's similarly tentative speculation that "Perhaps . . . Shakespeare's sensitivity to the status of the dead was intensified by the death in 1596 of his son Hamnet (a name virtually interchangeable with Hamlet in the period's public records) and still more perhaps by the death of his father, John, in 1601, the most likely year of the writing of *Hamlet*" (248).

4. Edmund Jabès, "To answer to . . . To answer for . . . ," in *In Relation: ACTS 10* (San Francisco, 1989), 28 (author's italics).

5. See Stephen Orgel's "absolutely basic question about our sense of Shakespearean drama: when we read the text of a play, what do we assume that text represents—what do we *see*? The simplest answer is that we see only words on a page" (*Imagining Shakespeare: A History of Texts*

and Visions [Houndsmills, England, and New York: Palgrave Macmillan, 2003], 1). Noting "the basic question of what a [Renaissance] book was conceived to be," Orgel makes a similar claim when he writes that, "One way of thinking of character is simply as part of the text. This of course is the original meaning of the word: both a written account of a person, and the letters—characters—in which the account is written. . . . " ("What Is a Character?" in *The Authentic Shakespeare: And Other Problems of the Early Modern Stage* [New York and London: Routledge, 2002], 7–8).

6. Michel Foucault, "What is An Author?" in *The Foucault Reader*, ed. Paul Rabinow, trans. Josué V. Harari (New York: Pantheon Books, 1984), 109. Given questions such as these, the question then becomes "how"—how do we find out "where [the text] come[s] from, who wrote it, when, under what circumstances." But whereas Foucault claims we cannot know such things (given "the effacement of the writing subject's individual characteristics" [102] as well as "the author's disappearance" [105]), David Scott Kastan proposes that criticism ("after theory") *can* answer Foucault's questions by confronting "the text's historicity, [which is] the very condition of its being, a historicity that locates creativity within determinate conditions of realization. Rather than seek to escape this full, complicating historicity by attempting to penetrate the text's signifying surface in search of the author's original intentions (admittedly, themselves a historical fact, however difficult to determine), we should energetically confront that surface, which is, in fact, the only place where the activity of literary production can be engaged. This is not to deny the creativity of the author but rather to understand it; for the material text is where the conditions and constraints of authorship become legible, where its authority is at once asserted and undermined, as the author's dependency upon other agents becomes obvious and the literary object reveals its inevitably multiple histories and significations—histories and significations that in fact extend beyond the text's verbal structure. All aspects of the text's materiality signify and its inescapable materiality is witness to the collaborative nature of the text and textuality" (*Shakespeare After Theory* [New York and London: Routledge, 1999], 32, 39–40).

7. "The Death of The Author," in *Image—Music—Text*, trans. Stephen Heath (New York: The Noonday Press, 1988), 143. See again Kastan, who wants (for criticism "after theory") "a set of interests and

procedures more rigorously historical than recent theory-driven studies have been": "The oft-proclaimed 'death of the author' might direct our efforts here, but not in the context of literary theory's insistence upon the text's defiant plurality of meaning. The notorious phrase becomes intelligible rather than merely provocative in the recovery of the actual discourses that circulate around and through the text as well as the historically specific conditions of its writing and circulation, both of which must inevitably compromise and disperse any simple notion of authorial intention. Both discursively and materially, authorship is revealed to be more problematic—that is, at once less single and more constrained—than our conventional notions of artistic autonomy and authorial intention would allow. . . . [T]he author is not autonomous and sovereign, neither the solitary source nor the sole proprietor of the meanings that circulate through the text. This is not to dismiss or denigrate the claims of authorship, only to observe that the act of writing is inevitably fettered and circumscribed. An author writes always and only within specific conditions and possibility, both institutional and imaginative, connecting the individual talent to preexisting modes of thought, linguistic rules, literary conventions, social codes, legal restraints, material practices, and commercial conditions of production" (31, 32–33). Compare David Quint's claim that "The text no longer seems to speak with a single voice of its own, the voice of an individual author with whom the reader might seek a common human understanding" ("Introduction," in *Literary Theory/Renaissance Texts*, ed. Patricia Parker and David Quint (Baltimore: Johns Hopkins University Press, 1986), 7).

8. See however Kastan, who argues that "The notion of such self-sufficiency demands an idealization of authorial intention that must find the material text always inadequate, a defective version of what is imagined. Rather, the work of literature might better be understood as an actual product of an author working in (and against) specific discursive and institutional circumstances; and literary study, in turn, might better be defined not as the uncovering of the author's uniquely privileged meaning concealed somehow within the text but as the discovery of the text itself as it speaks the corporate activities that have brought it into being, the 'complex social practices,' as Margreta de Grazia and Peter Stallybrass write [in "The Materiality of the Shakespearean Text," *Shakespeare Quarterly* 44 (1993), 283)], 'that shaped, and still shape [its] absorbent surface'" (38).

9. Foucault, 102–3. See also Foucault's claim that "We find the link between writing and death manifested in the total effacement of the individual characteristics of the writer. . . . If we wish to know the writer in our day, it will be through the singularity of his absence and in his link to death, which has transformed him into a victim of his own writing" (*Language, Counter-Memory, Practice,* ed. and trans. Donald F. Bouchard [Ithaca: Cornell University Press 1977], 117; quoted in Garber, 12).

10. See for example John Crowe Ransom, "Criticism Inc.," *The Virginia Quarterly Review,* Autumn, 1937, 586-602; repr. in *The World's Body* (New York: Charles Scribner's Sons, 1938) and William K. Wimsatt and Monroe C. Beardsley, "The Intentional Fallacy," *Sewanee Review* 54.3, Summer, 1946; repr. in *The Verbal Icon: Studies in the Meaning of Poetry* (Lexington: University of Kentucky Press, 1954).

11. Barthes, 42. Compare Jacques Derrida's claim that "By definition, a written signature implies the actual or empirical nonpresence of the signer" ("Signature, Event, Context," in *Margins of Philosophy,* trans. Alan Bass [Chicago: University of Chicago Press, 1982], 328).

12. See for instance Murray Schwartz and Coppélia Kahn, who claim that "Shakespeare's central subject is the formation and contexts of the very identity he seems at once to lack and to exemplify. . . . His plays and poems do not merely illustrate his identity but are in each instance a dynamic expression of the struggle to re-create and explore its origins and consequences" ("Introduction," in *Representing Shakespeare: New Psychoanalytic Essays,* ed. Murray M. Schwartz and Coppélia Kahn [Baltimore: Johns Hopkins University Press, 1980], xv–xvi).

13. Letter to George and Tom Keats, 21 December, 1817. *The Letters of John Keats,* ed. Maurice Buxton Forman (London and New York: Oxford University Press, 1931), 72.

14. "Constructing Inwardness as Privacy, or Representing the Unrepresented in Early Modern Culture," Keynote Address at The Arts and Public Policy Conference ("Private Lives and Public Roles: Literature and the Arts 1500–1700"), University of Central Florida, March 26, 1993.

15. "The Sound of O in Othello," in *The Subjectivity Effect in Western Literary Tradition: Essays Toward the Release of Shakespeare's Will* (Cambridge, Mass.: The MIT Press, 1991), 143–64.

16. Foucault, 119–20.

Index

absence, and presence, 156n3,
163n15; of author, xvi, 105–6,
110, 113, 173n9; of female
performers, 126n3; of objective
correlative, 129n10; of offstage
action, xiv, xviii, 43, 77, 93, 105,
129n10; of penis, 155n3; of
Shakespeare, 105–6
acting, as form of oratory, 128n8
action, absence of, xiv, xviii, 43,
77, 93, 105, 129–30n12; as
erotic activity, 125–26n3; as
physical gestures, 4, 7, 25,
27–28, 31–32, 128n8, 155n3;
described in words, xv, xvii, xix,
18, 24, 37, 56, 64, 66, 72, 77,
84, 101, 128n9, 147n2, 153n13,
165–66n28; disappearance
into words of, xi, xv, xvii;
improbability of, 5, 129n11;
indistinguishable from words,
xvi; mimesis in words of, xii;

not performed physically, xi–xii,
xvi–xviii, 2–9, 11–12, 14–19,
21–22, 25, 32, 34, 36–39,
41–3, 45, 50, 55, 59, 62, 73,
81–83, 86, 94, 96, 98, 100, 102,
105–6, 111, 125–27nn3, 5,
127n11; painted in words, xvi, ;
performance of, 3–4, 14–15, 76,
78, 94; remembered in words,
28, 84; seamlessness of words
and, xii; unnoticed words like
unseen, 66, 70, 98, 136n2. *See
also* hearing, seeing, sound
actor, and audience, xiii–xiv, 3–5,
9–10, 25, 33–34, 37, 41, 51,
79, 121–22n7; and physical
gestures, 7, 27; and reader, 5;
as boy playing woman's part,
107, 126n3, 156n3; as character,
5; as embodiment of words,
128–29n9; in Shakespeare's
company, 25, 121–22n7; like

STEPHEN RATCLIFFE is a poet and critic whose most recent book is *REAL*, a 474-page serial poem written in 474 consecutive days (Avenue B, 2007). Previous books include *Portraits & Repetition* (The Post-Apollo Press, 2002) and *SOUND/(system)* (Green Integer, 2002). *Listening to Reading*, a collection of essays on contemporary experimental poetry, was published by SUNY Press in 2000. He is also the author of *Campion: On Song* (Routledge & Kegan Paul, 1981). He lives in Bolinas, California, and teaches at Mills College in Oakland.